Delacroix

Phoebe Pool

Delacroix

The Colour Library of Art

Paul Hamlyn

London · New York · Sydney · Toronto

Acknowledgments

The paintings in this book are reproduced by kind permission of the following collections, galleries and museums to which they belong: Ajaccio Cathedral, Corsica (Plate 5); Albright-Knox Art Gallery, Buffalo, New York (Plate 19); M. Leonardo Benatov, Paris (Plate 4); M. Marcel Beurdeley, Paris (Plate 42); Bibliothèque Nationale, Paris (Frontispiece Figure 1); City Museum and Art Gallery, Birmingham (Plate 21); Sterling and Francine Clark Art Institute, Williamstown, Massachusetts (Figure 4); Church of Saint Sulpice, Paris (Plate 49); Fogg Art Museum, Harvard University, Cambridge, Massachusetts, Gift of Meta and Paul J. Sachs (Figure 5); Jerome Hill Collection, New York (Plate 26); Musée des Augustans, Toulouse (Plate 36); Musée des Beaux-Arts, Bordeaux (Plates 14, 17, 45); Musée des Beaux-Arts, Lille (Plate 31); Musée des Beaux-Arts de Lyon (Plate 15); Musée des Beaux-Arts, Nancy (Plate 18); Musée des Beaux-Arts de Nantes (Plate 24); Musée Carnavalet, Paris (Plate 40); Musée d'Ordrupgaard, Copenhagen, Hansen Collection (Plate 28); Musée National du Louvre, Paris (Plates 2, 3, 6, 8, 13, 16, 20, 22, 23, 25, 29, 30, 32, 33, 35, 46, Figures 2, 3); Museum of Fine Arts, Springfield, Massachusetts (Plate 10); Dr. Fritz Nathan Collection, Zurich (Plate 43); National Gallery, London (Plates 11, 41, 47); Palais Bourbon, Paris (Plate 34); Palais du Luxembourg, Paris (Plate 37); Phillips Collection, Washington (Plate 48); Private Collection (Plate 1); Royal Museum of Fine Arts, Brussels (Plate 39); Dr. W.F. Schnyder, Solothurn (Plate 9); Staatsgalerie Stuttgart (Plate 44); E.V. Thaw Collection, New York (Plate 38); Toledo Museum of Fine Art, Gift of Thomas A. de Vilbiss (Plate 27); Wallace Collection, London (Plate 12); The Lord and Lady Walston Collection, Cambridge (Plate 7).

The following photographs were supplied by: A.C.L., Brussels (Plate 39); Albright-Knox Art Gallery, Buffalo, New York (Plate 19); Agraci, Paris (Plate 18); Henry B. Beville, Virginia (Plate 48); Bibliothèque Nationale (Frontispiece, Figure 1); Camponagara, Lyon (Plate 15); Sterling and Francine Clark Art Institute, Williamstown, Massachusetts (Figure 4); Alain Danvers, Bordeaux (Plates 17, 45); Walter Drayer, Zurich (Plate 43); Editions Cercle d'Art, Paris (Plate 1); Fogg Art Museum, Cambridge, Massachusetts (Figure 5); Giraudon, Paris (Plates 5, 8, 14, 22, 24, 31, 33, 49); Jerome Hill, New York (Plate 26); Michael Holford, London (Plates 12, 13); Raymond Laniepce, Paris (2, 3, 4, 6, 16, 20, 23, 25, 29, 30, 32, 35, 40, 42, 46); Musée d'Ordrupgaard, Copenhagen (Plate 28); Museum of Fine Arts, Springfield, Massachusetts (Plate 10); National Gallery, London (Plates 11, 41, 47); Eric Pollitzer, New York (Plate 38); Réalités, Paris (Figure 1); Reilly and Constantine, Birmingham (Plate 21); Dr. W.F. Schnyder, Solothurn (Plate 9); Service du Documentation, Versailles (Figures 2, 3); Staatsgalerie, Stuttgart (Plate 44); Stearn and Sons (Cambridge) Ltd. (Plate 7); Thames and Hudson Limited, London (Plates 34, 37); Toledo Museum of Fine Art (Plate 27); Yan, Toulouse (Plate 36).

Frontispiece: Daguerreotype of Delacroix taken in 1832.

Published by The Hamlyn Publishing Group Limited
London · New York · Sydney · Toronto
Hamlyn House, Feltham, Middlesex, England
© Copyright 1969 The Hamlyn Publishing Group Limited
Printed in Italy by Officine Grafiche Arnoldo Mondadori, Verona

Contents

2 Study for *The Moroccan Blacksmith*. 1853.

Introduction

EUGÈNE DELACROIX was one of those painters like Gauguin whose impact on history was probably greater than their actual artistic achievement. 'We are all in Delacroix,' said Paul Cézanne, who produced an apotheosis of the master sailing up to the heavens, like some Baroque saint of modern painting. This feeling of respect was not confined to the Impressionist generation, to Renoir, Degas, Monet and Pissarro, but extended also to their successors Van Gogh, Seurat and Gauguin, although they were often highly critical of the intervening taste for realism. Delacroix could make a double appeal to posterity, at first as an original and experimental colourist with a semi-scientific interest in natural effects (Dr Lee Johnson has concentrated on this aspect of his talents in a recent monograph) and later, to Gauguin's generation, as a pioneer of the more musical and Baudelairean concepts of painting, painting which should derive from 'the mysterious centre of thought'. During his lifetime his friend George Sand rightly insisted on this complexity, observing that 'through his many-sided intelligence' he was able to appreciate 'the varied aspects of beauty'. It is the same complexity which makes it difficult to enrol under any one label this lover of Classical antiquity who could ridicule David, this Romantic who stressed unity and preferred Mozart to Berlioz and Chopin. Some writers such as René Huyghe have attempted to escape the dilemma by putting him in a third category — that of the dandy.

Delacroix was probably the last great painter who, unlike Courbet and Manet, felt no continued obligation either to be of his own time or to depict it. When he speaks of modernity he seems to be alluding not to the external scene but to a mood of nervosity and melancholy; thus he declared Mozart to be modern — 'that is to say he is not afraid to touch on the melancholy side of things'. Perhaps the nearest he came towards recognising a specifically modern task was to write: 'We live in a time of despondency. Courage is needed to make a god of a beauty which is unquiet'. But nevertheless without Delacroix, contemporary Romanticism, with all its ferocity and gloom, its passion for medievalism and for English and Oriental themes, would not have found a worthy interpretation in paint. Even the sensible Taine noticed this: 'Bear in mind that he said something new and the one thing which we needed.' But Delacroix neglected one Romantic theme dear to contemporary Englishmen and Germans — the emotional bond between the poet or painter and the world of 'nature' outside him. He rarely painted landscapes without figures, although when he did, these are amongst his most moving works.

Delacroix was born in 1798, early enough, like the older Stendhal, for him to glimpse the heroic tumult of the Empire. He could never acclimatize himself to the more tame and bourgeois age of Louis-Philippe and to the money grubbers described by Stendhal and by Flaubert in *L'Education Sentimentale* (1846-69), who would have sold themselves and France at the drop of a hat. He belonged to the world of Beethoven and Kant's Idealism when it was still possible to speculate about the nature of art in a wide and metaphysical way. (He seems to have read some of Kant's aesthetics which were as much in harmony with his own ideas as Comte's materialism was suited to the circle of Courbet.) His idea of history, like that of Michelet, was a matter of stormy crowds and dramatic incident rather than the semi-scientific enquiry into race or climate which interested Taine. Delacroix was born well before the disillusion and cynicism engendered by the failure of the 1848 rising. His high seriousness would not have permitted him to call his pictures his 'articles' as Degas did. Degas and Manet's generation were far more wary of the big certitudes, less inclined to believe in a lofty struggle between the forces of humanity and darkness which is the implicit subject matter of Delacroix's murals. (It might have been difficult successfully to undertake a large mural programme without some such noble conception of man and his destiny, which was shared in their different ways by Puvis de Chavannes and by Théodore Chenavard, who devised the abortive scheme for a secularized Pantheon.) Delacroix also lived before the full impact of Positivism and of Realism which was in part its child. If he read Baudelaire's plea for a 'painter of modern life' it came too late to affect his art. None of the critics who dispute as to whether he was a Romantic or a Classical painter has ever tried to enrol him under the banner of Realism.

The view that Delacroix began as a Romantic and then became Classical (beginning with his discovery of the living Antiquity, the Arab Catos and Brutuses who he saw in Africa and Tangiers) is over-simplified and untrue. The two strands of romanticism and classicism were intermixed in his nature from the beginning. He had an orthodox, rational and classical education at the Lycée Louis le Grand, later attended by Edgar Degas. A few years ago some of his school note-books were discovered, and from these we learn that he read Homer, Virgil, Horace and Marcus Aurelius together with the principal French classics including Voltaire. He wrote later: 'I know the Ancients, that is to say I have learnt to put them above everything.' This admiration was no doubt confirmed by the teaching in the studio of David's pupil, Guérin, and Delacroix's own followers tell us that he never mentioned Guérin without affection and respect. When, in 1821, he was commissioned to decorate the actor Talma's dining room, the studies he made for this, as Lee Johnson has shown, were taken mainly from Classical statues and bas reliefs in the Louvre and from engravings of Greco-Roman paintings together with a few French Classical decorations. Unlike Ingres, he seems not to have admired the linear abstraction of Greek vase painting and of Flaxman which was entirely opposed to his own technique of drawing from the central mass outwards. His great feeling for Raphael is apparent in the two early church decorations — *The Virgin of the Harvest* (1819) in the Church at Orcement and *The Virgin of the Sacred Heart* (plate 5). Even in 1830, the year of *Hernani*, he was undogmatic enough to contribute a laudatory article on Raphael to *Le Revue de Paris*. In mid-career too, in some mature pictures of his family and friends, he seems to have been capable of switching back to the Neo-Davidian style which he had used for his early portraits (plates 1 and 21).

On the other hand, Delacroix had many qualities in common with his Romantic contemporaries — his melancholy, his love of solitude and the countryside, the fascination which he felt for violence and bloodshed. In May 1824 he wrote in his journal, which was not intended for public consumption: 'I have no love for reasonable painting. There is in me an old leaven, some black depth which must be appeased. If I am not quivering and excited like a serpent in the hands of a soothsayer I am uninspired.' He complained later in life that others, not he himself, had enrolled him under the Romantic banner. But he also admitted: 'If by my Romanticism they mean the free manifestation of my personal impressions, my effort to get away from the types eternally copied in the schools and my dislike of academic recipes – then I admit that not only am I a Romantic, but also have been one since I was fifteen, when I already preferred Prud'hon and Gros to Guérin and Girodet.' In order to inspire himself he would often read certain passages from Byron, particularly from *The Giaour* and the end of *The Bride of Abydos*.

Delacroix's early note-books also show that Romantic interest in medieval subjects which later led him to paint *The Battle of Poitiers* and many themes from Scott and Dumas. A feeling for the Middle Ages had become increasingly fashionable in France since the beginning of the century, when Chateaubriand published his *Génie du Christianisme*. Already at Delacroix's lycée such themes were set for composition as Joan of Arc's speech to the English. (L'Ecole de Chartres had been founded to study the Middle Ages, and women went to dances dressed as Queen Frédégonde.) Delacroix's medievalism, however, was expressed more in themes than in his style. He felt no wish to emulate the Primitives, French or Italian, and did not share Ingres's taste for Fra Angelico and Botticelli — a taste which André Chastel has shown to be comparatively widespread. On the contrary, Delacroix said that to copy these early artists was like grown men imitating the prattle of childhood.

Delacroix was helped to liberate himself from the somewhat constricting tradition of Raphael and David by the example of two contemporaries — Théodore Géricault and the Baron Antoine-Jean Gros. When he first saw the former's *Raft of the Medusa* (1819) Delacroix reports: 'The impression it made on me was so vivid that I ran like a madman all the way back to the Rue de la Planche.' In the light of Delacroix's later, more atmospheric works, *The Raft* appears sullen and livid in colour and excessively sculptural. Nor did the mature Delacroix approve Géricault's way of building up a picture piecemeal from a squared-up design, for he believed that even from the beginning it must be treated as a unity: 'However unfinished a picture may be, everything must have its relative importance.' But Géricault's intensity — the frenzy contained within a comparatively orthodox compositional form — must have been very sympathetic to him. It has lately been fashionable to minimise the influence of Géricault on Delacroix, but the latter must have assimilated much of his friend's manner, for in 1864, when the contents of Delacroix's studio were sold, there was already some doubt as to whether certain copies were by one or the other artist.

Géricault's influence on Delacroix is most obvious in *The Barque of Dante* (plate 6), exhibited at the Salon in 1822, which, although organised in David-like Neo-Classical planes parallel to the surface, is painted in dark Caravaggio-like colours with flesh-tones very near to those of the crew of the *Medusa*. The large, monumental figures brought close to the spectator are like Géricault's, and so is the theme of a heavily laden boat, which recurs constantly in Delacroix's later work. It is possible, too, that Géricault's example inspired Delacroix's two themes drawn from contemporary life, the *Massacre at Chios* and *Liberty Leading the People*. For the first of these he questioned an eye-witness (see note) as Géricault had done, and he himself may have witnessed a scene in the July Revolution which he idealised into the picture of Liberty. But Delacroix did not pursue the theme of modern life as it seems Géricault, had he lived, might have done. After Stendhal and Géricault this subject went underground for a while, and was revived by Baudelaire and the circle around Courbet. This must have been one of the few ways in which Delacroix disappointed the admiring Baudelaire.

We have already noted Delacroix's assertion that at fifteen he preferred Prud'hon and Gros to the Neo-Classical Guérin and Girodet. Gros had himself been a student of David, but his mature works served rather to undermine than support the Neo-Classical tradition; he painted not antique sagas, but contemporary violence — the Napoleonic campaigns which he saw at first hand. Moreover, he preferred moving to statuesque figures, and adopted Rubens's fluid painting technique and sensuous colours. In an essay of 1840, Delacroix especially praised Gros's horses, which, he said, had a rare mixture of force and elegance, and were even more noble and spirited than those of Rubens. In a dynamic sketch for *Bucephalus vanquished by Alexander*, Gros heralded those favourite subjects of Delacroix — a rearing horse intertwined with its rider, or two animals fighting. Gros showed Delacroix the way to Rubens, who, with Veronese, was probably the main influence on Delacroix's mature work, especially on the vast mural decorations. There are passages in *The Barque*

3 Delacroix and his friends on New Year's Eve. 1817.

of Dante reminiscent of Rubens's *Landing of Marie de Medici* in the Louvre. (Delacroix later said that the small speckles of bright colour on the bodies in the water, his first attempt to produce sparkling light in this way, were inspired by studying Rubens.) It was gratifying that Gros should be the man to describe the *Dante* as a 'chastened Rubens'.

Like many other great artists of the 19th century, including Degas, Renoir, and Cézanne, Delacroix copied Old Masters in the Louvre, as a substitute for the technical training which had once been provided by the painters' workshops and guilds, and because they found the teaching of such masters as Guérin and Gleyre inadequate for their needs. Amongst other works Delacroix copied Veronese's *Marriage at Cana* and Giorgione's *Fête Champêtre*. He knew Titian's *Presentation of the Virgin* from engravings; it formed the compositional framework of his *Return of Columbus*. The journal tells us that he longed to unite the style of Michelangelo and Velasquez, but in fact most of his compositions, particularly the murals, owed more to the Venetian colourist tradition, which stressed the musical harmony of the whole, than to the more linear and anatomical particularism of Michelangelo and the Florentines, which he later critized for lack of unity.

From his early years Delacroix had been attracted by the East. This was a widespread taste, a romantic feeling for the exotic stimulated by Bonaparte's Egyptian campaigns. His contemporary Decamps painted Indians and Eugène Fromentin, the critic and novelist, portrayed the North African scene with a delicate restraint. Delacroix's school note-books have sketches of men in Turkish costume. Later he used to visit the painter Auguste and borrow from his collection of Eastern clothes and swords, and in the 20s he made copies from Persian miniatures. Byron's poems, *The Giaour*, *Lara*, and *The Bride of Abydos*, and still more the poet's death in Greece, heightened this feeling. The French Liberals sided vociferously with Greece in the war against Turkey, and when in 1822 about twenty thousand Greeks were massacred on the island of Chios, Delacroix immediately realised that this must be his next subject for the Salon, although he was not shattered by the news as Picasso was by the bombing of Guernica. Gros had provided precedents for scenes of modern warfare, particularly in his *Napoleon Visiting the Victims of the Plague at Jaffa*, but this was considered by the critics and public as a less shocking subject than Delacroix's, in that the presence of the merciful Napoleon was thought to have ennobled and raised the theme. Although Delacroix again arranged his figures in the form of a Neo-Classical frieze (plate 8), his sketches and studies show the composition growing more dynamic as it developed. (As Delacroix wrote 'My picture is gaining a torsion, an energetic movement which I absolutely must complete'.) The background was originally to be closed in, following the somewhat airless and box-like tradition of David, but this was changed to give a greater sense of distance and atmosphere.

At first Delacroix was taken up with combining 'a firm yet melting impasto' with strong, bold contours; he also wished the picture to contain 'that fine black, that fortunate muddiness' which he admired in Velasquez, and in a Spanish portrait which he was then copying in the belief that it was by this master. But after seeing Constable's *Hay Wain* at a dealer's (it was to be shown in the Salon of 1824), Delacroix so much admired the sparkle of reflected light Constable had achieved by tiny patches of flickering paint, that he re-touched and enlivened his own picture, particularly in the foreground, by applying small speckles of blue, orange and pink dots, and the use of scumbling and of varnish instead of oil. Contemporary accounts differ as to how much he altered and when, but there is little doubt that he did so. At this time he noted that looking at Constable's pictures did him a power of good, and later, in 1847: 'Constable says that the

superiority of the green in his fields is due to its being made up of a multitude of different greens, juxtaposed not mixed.' In the additions to the *Massacre of Chios*, one can see the beginning of Delacroix's later interest in 'liaison', which he calls 'that art, those reflections which form a whole of objects most disparate in colour'.

Less than a year after exhibiting *The Massacre of Chios*, Delacroix paid a visit of three months to England, a country connected with his early love-affairs, with Géricault, with his friends Richard Parkes Bonington and the Fielding brothers, and with the Romantic writings of Scott and Byron. It was a period of general Anglophilia, partly stimulated by the returning emigrés. Parisian dandies admired Brummell and wore English dress, horse-racing *à l'Anglaise* was fashionable and Kemble and Kean took the town by storm with their performances of Shakespeare; the Duchesse de Berry gave a vast Marie Stuart ball at the Tuileries. Géricault had returned from London in 1820 considerably excited by English paintings, particularly perhaps by the animal paintings of Ward. His enthusiasm was shared by the many minor artists who followed him there, partly in search of their own artistic tradition, from which they felt separated by the French Revolution and the Neo-Classical rigours of David. Although Delacroix's visit to London did not revolutionise his art, the influence of English painting is very apparent in his work for the next five years. (The effect was probably prolonged by seeing a great deal of Bonington on his return.) Delacroix was delighted to find more freedom, brio and brightness in a country where Rubens was studied more as a matter of course than as an act of defiance. Even in his old age he still advised French painters to study the English because, he said, it was a young and not an ageing country.

Delacroix had already been initiated into the English technique of watercolour painting by the anglicised Soulier and by Thales Fielding, with whom he shared a studio in

1823. Watercolour suited his taste for fluid painting rather than for the tight manner of the Neo-Classical school. The Louvre has his sketch-book of 1825, in which some of the watercolours (in particular certain views of Greenwich and Brighton) executed with great brilliance of technique, closely resemble those of Constable. (It is only fair to say that the writing on one of these is not by Delacroix, and the painting's authenticity has been doubted by Douglas Cooper.) In the pictures which followed the English visit Delacroix also began to use far more rich glazes and bright golds and reds — all practices more usual in England than France.

Delacroix kept no journal in England, but fortunately letters to his friends Pierret and Soulier reflect his new impressions. He found the music atrocious, and thought London lacked any feeling for architecture. He relished 'a sort of savagery and fierceness' in the *canaille* as well as 'the noblest' politeness and dandyism of the upper classes. On the whole, he reflected: 'There is something sad and uncouth in all this, which does not fit in with what we have in France'. He was sorry not to see Turner or Constable, who were both away, but Sir Thomas Lawrence, 'the most gracious of men except when anyone criticized his pictures', received him very kindly. Delacroix particularly admired the way in which Lawrence painted women's eyes and half-opened mouths. Reminiscences of Lawrence's works have often been pointed out in the portrait of Baron Schwiter (plate 11) and those of Delacroix's relations, the Verninacs. The easy pose and bravura of the *Schwiter*, the Baron's stance and somewhat rippling outline against the garden background, and the light which plays along the bridge of the nose, owe something to Lawrence's portrait of the Duke of Wellington. The glossy blacks and highlights in Delacroix's pictures at this time are like Lawrence's, and the Verninacs seem to step almost out of the canvas in the manner of the Waterloo portraits.

Delacroix found Wilkie's sketches better than his finished portraits, and an oil sketch for the Englishman's *John Knox Preaching before the Lords of Congregation* seems to have left traces in *The Murder of the Bishop of Liège*. Here, too, the background was English, apparently taken from sketches made by Delacroix in Westminster Hall. Etty's picture of *The Storm* may have contributed something to Delacroix's many versions of *Christ on the Sea of Galilee*, and the blonde nudes may be echoed in the sumptuous women who sprawl over the death-bed of Sardanapalus.

The most impassioned phrases in the letters home are reserved for the superb performances of Shakespeare which in England were, apparently, more unrestrained, less emasculated and sweetened than the French versions. Delacroix preferred Kean's wild outbursts to the more moderate acting of Young. He attended a considerable number of Shakespeare's plays, including *Richard III*, *The Tempest*, *Othello*, and *The Merchant of Venice*, which all furnished him with themes for later paintings or lithographs. It was characteristic of Delacroix's period to have this taste for drama and rhetoric, while the realist generation of Degas and Manet preferred the documentary novel, which was more akin to the off-beat, more casual and ordinary moments of life which they tried to depict.

Delacroix also found in England the idea for his *Horse Terrified by a Storm* which was probably inspired by a picture of Sawtrey Gilpin as well as by Géricault. The background of *The Natchez* (plate 7) painted before the English visit, is somewhat like landscapes of Constable, and the theme of *The Penance of Jane Shore* (plate 9) must be derived from a translation of the English play. Delacroix owned engravings of the Tower of London menagerie, and his pictures of animals were also indebted to Stubbs, Ward and Landseer.

Delacroix had, of course, read some of Byron's poetry before he went to England (probably in the translation of André Pichot). In 1824 he was already reminding himself of a recipe for inspiration: 'Always excite your imagination by remembering certain passages from Byron,' and amongst these he specified the death of Hassan from *The Giaour* — in fact six canvases treat this favoured subject. In England he probably saw and was influenced by the lithographs of Cruikshank and Stothard illustrating Byron. (Professor Heard Hamilton has traced several motifs apparently borrowed from the Englishmen, most clearly in *The Prisoner of Chillon*.) Delacroix's lithographs of Faust may well have been inspired by an adaptation of this legend for the stage in England, perhaps Marlowe's *Dr Faustus*.

Richard Parkes Bonington would no doubt have been congenial to Delacroix as a painter, even apart from his personal charm which Delacroix noticed in 1816 when he encountered in the Louvre 'a tall adolescent in a short jacket making studies in water-colour from the Flemish landscapes'. They saw most of each other in the years immediately after Delacroix's visit to England, and according to Lee Johnson, there is some evidence that they studied Venetian painting together. Bonington could be coarse and flashy in his use of glitter and slippery highlights, but he showed great dexterity, variety and freedom in his actual handling of paint. The composition and the chiaroscuro of his *Francis I and Marguerite of Navarre* are superior to Delacroix's comparable work (also in the Wallace Collection) *Faust and Mephistopheles*. At the end of his life, years after Bonington was dead, Delacroix described in a letter his friend's 'lightness of execution which, especially in the water-colour medium, seems to turn his pictures into diamonds, independently of any subject which they may represent'. Bonington was partly responsible perhaps for the dazzling colour used by Delacroix at this time; we know that he made copies of the Englishman's pictures. In *The Execution of Doge Marino Faliero* (plate 12) exhibited at the Salon of 1827, Delacroix has set his figures against the pure white of the Scala dei Giganti,

which is also the main setting in a picture by a follower of Bonington. Delacroix probably recognized the affinities of his work with the contemporary English school, for he sent *Marino Faliero* to London, where it was particularly admired by Sir Thomas Lawrence, who even considered buying it. At this time, too, Delacroix wrote to his friend Soulier: 'Bonington has been for some time in my studio. I regret you are not with us. There is much to learn from the society of that rascal'.

Another work apparently owing something to Delacroix's English visit is the *Still Life with Lobsters* (1827) where the red coats of men hunting in a green plain are echoed in the tartan stripes on the game bag. At this time he also painted several small odalisques in brilliant colours, the most dazzling of which is the *Woman with a Parrot* at Lyons (plate 15). But his most famous nudes appear in the much derided Salon picture *The Death of Sardanapalus*, inspired by a play of Byron.

Delacroix himself sometimes had misgivings about this picture, which he called 'an Asiatic feat of arms against David's Spartiate pastiche'. The composition is no longer organised in a frieze or pyramid with a definite axis as *The Barque of Dante* had been, but in a great sweeping diagonal reinforced by converging lines which direct the eye to Sardanapalus at the top left-hand corner. The exuberant colour and dynamic movement owe more to Rubens than had any of the earlier works. Even more than *The Massacre of Chios*, the *Sardanapalus* merits Baudelaire's description — 'a hymn of woe to irreparable grief'. It can be seen either as a manifesto of militant Romanticism or as Delacroix's farewell to the dreams of his youth. After this he turned towards cooler tones and more concentrated composition. But even in *Sardanapalus* there are traces of Classicism; as Lee Johnson has pointed out, the composition is partly based on an engraving of a pseudo-Etruscan relief, which also depicts a slaughter. There are some magnificent studies for this picture, some in oil, some in pastel. (Delacroix told Andrieu that he was trying to reproduce blonde tonality of pastel.)

Between 1828 and 1832 Delacroix generally used more sombre colours and chiaroscuro to unify his compositions; this may have been partly due to the practice of lithography and to the discovery about this time of Rembrandt's painting. The lithographs were of subjects taken from *Faust*, by which Delacroix was haunted after seeing a version of it on the London stage. Goethe generously said that these illustrations 'surpassed my own pictures of the scenes', and noticed that Delacroix had 'in this dark work assimilated all the gloom inherent in its original composition'. In 1828 Delacroix also made a lithograph of Hamlet with Yorick's skull, an anticipation of the whole series on the Prince of Denmark which was executed in 1834. As Delacroix at this time was passing through one of his recurrent stages of discouragement and gloom, it is understandable that he should have concerned himself with two tortured minds. In his letters he described himself as overwhelmed with sadness and boredom: 'I no longer find the same charm in things. Alas, there is a prism of enchantment which gradually loses its colour.'

At this time Delacroix painted several pictures with historical subjects in style somewhat reminiscent of Gros, particularly when he is depicting snowy battlefields, as in *The Battle of Nancy* (plate 18). Here small figures sweep through vast backgrounds, and Delacroix uses a fluid chiaroscuro to break the isolation of the individual bodies and bind them together. He admired the dense shadows and vagueness he found in Rembrandt, and made use of similar effects in *The Murder of the Bishop of Liège* (1829) and *Boissy d'Anglas at the Convention* (plate 17). Gautier describes the seething confusion in the former: 'Who would ever have thought that anyone could paint tumult? Movement, yes; but this not enormously large picture howls, shouts and blasphemes.'

Apart from *The Massacre of Chios* and *Greece Expiring on the Ruins of Missolonghi*, Delacroix's only work inspired by contemporary history was *Liberty Leading the People* (plate 16), an idealization of the July Revolution in 1830. Delacroix, a fastidious aristocrat, generally distrusted explosions of popular feeling, but at this time he probably felt that a renewal of art would go hand in hand with an increase in political liberty. He had heartily disliked the government of Charles X which refused to buy any of his works (the new government bought this picture and gave the painter the Légion d'Honneur). Delacroix had joined the Garde Nationale, and may have watched some fighting near the river similar to the scene which he painted. In composition *Liberty Leading the People* is a development from *Greece Expiring* (plate 14), which also has a large symbolical figure surmounting dead bodies, the whole forming a triangular construction. But in the later picture there is a more brilliant use of colour and chiaroscuro and a more dynamic movement both upwards and forwards. Delacroix has found formal means to express the idealism and irresistible onrush of the rebels. The figure of Liberty owes something to the *Venus de Milo* discovered in 1820 and first shown in the Louvre during the following year; it has been suggested that with this figure Delacroix was trying to outdo the antique Victory in *The Apotheosis of Homer* by Ingres. He may also have been inspired by Auguste Barbier's poem on the July days:

> 'Liberty is not a countess
> From the noble St. Germain district...
> She is a strong woman with powerful breasts'

By the time of the 1848 rising, Delacroix's liberal sympathies had worn very thin: 'I have buried the man I used to be', he wrote.

The invitation to accompany Comte de Mornay on a diplomatic mission to Morocco in 1832 was perhaps the most fortunate event in Delacroix's life. It came when he was somewhat depressed, bored with fashionable Paris and perhaps a little sated with themes of odalisques and dark seething battles which had recently almost monopolised his attention. The notes and sketches made on this journey provided him with subjects which he was using right up to the time of his death -— horses fighting, whirling dervishes, Moroccan chiefs and Algerian women. His records, many of which are preserved, have been compared for their thoroughness and precision with those which Flaubert made for *Salammbô*.

The conditions were far from easy for a sensitive man; at Meknes, for example, the appearance of a Christian was so much loathed by the people that he always had to be escorted by a soldier. Even then the crowds reviled him as an infidel and pulled unpleasant faces.

Delacroix often mistrusted actuality and the living model, fearing that it would detract from the ideal, the work of the imagination. 'It is from the cruel reality of objects that I am trying to escape when I take refuge in artistic creation,' he wrote to Pierret in 1818. With his bias towards

> 'old unhappy far-off things
> and battles long ago'

he was at first almost stunned by 'the living, emphatic sublime, which fills the streets here and assassinates you with its reality... I am finding that sensations wear out in the long run, and the picturesque assaults your eye so strongly at every step that in the end one becomes insensitive to it.' One is reminded of Degas in New Orleans, apprehensive (and with as little justification) that the crowd of new impressions would lead not to art but merely to the immediacy of a photograph. But without losing his exhilaration Delacroix began to feel more at home: 'Perhaps a confused memory of the southern sunshine which I saw as a small child is

awakening in me.' (His father had been Prefect at Marseilles.) In Morocco, for once, actuality matched the ideals conceived in his imagination, and he was able to strike a balance between the two.

The brilliant light gave him better opportunities of studying colour, reflections and shadows than he had enjoyed in the north. (Monet found this, too, when, partly from admiration of Delacroix, he chose to do his military service in Africa.) 'The sea a deep fig-like blue-green, the hedges yellow on top because of the bamboos green at the bottom... shadow of white objects filled with blue reflections; red of the saddles and turban, almost black', he would note. A sheet in the back of one of his North Africa note-books has a rough colour triangle which seems to derive from the chemist Chevreul's studies of complementary colours, and underneath it Delacroix has observed that to add black to a colour only dirties it, it does not create a half-tone, which should be made by adding the complementary colour, thus neutralizing it. He also notes that a man with a yellow complexion will have violet shadows, one with a reddish complexion green shadows. Delacroix may have added this to the North African note-book at a later date, but certainly in 1833-4, when he was painting *Women of Algiers* (plate 20), he had far more interest in documentary realism than he had hitherto shown. The picture was put together largely from drawings made on the spot; and on a pastel study for the woman at the left Delacroix has noted that the skirt is more red at the turning of the folds and more violet in the parts which are less lighted. On a cushion Delacroix has fused red and green brushstrokes while the paint was still wet, in order to show the greying effect of the light on the local colour. But, as one would expect, realism is tempered by the demands of harmony; for example, a pink flower on the black headdress of the woman to the right does not appear in the sketches made on the spot, and was perhaps added to repeat the pink

4 Two Seated Moors in Conversation. 1832.

of the bodice. This evocation of a graceful, unhurried way of living might be cited as a pictorial equivalent of Baudelaire's

> 'Là tout n'est qu'ordre et beauté,
> Luxe, calme et volupté,'

had not Baudelaire himself discovered there the melancholy which he was almost always able to find (or invent): 'This aura of melancholy surrounds even the most engaging and showy of his pictures. That little poem of an interior, all silence and repose, and crammed with rich stuffs and knick-knacks of the toilet, seems somehow to exhale the heady scent of the brothel, which quickly enough guides one's thoughts towards the fathomless limbo of sadness'. But Baudelaire could be wrong about Delacroix, which perhaps explains the exasperation of his over-interpreted hero.

Both Delacroix's romantic and classical leanings were satisfied and fused by the Moroccan scene. In his article on Prud'hon he had derided the Neo-Classical school for 'its strange hatred of the resources of the picturesque in painting. Here the picturesque, the exotic, the remote were amply displayed, but at the same time the grave and dignified Arabs in their cloaks and toga-like burnous seemed a reincarnation of Antiquity: 'The Romans and Greeks are at my door: I have laughed a good deal at David's Greeks, apart of course from his sublime technique. I know them now; the marbles are truthful, but one must know how to read what they have to say, and our poor moderns have seen in them nothing but hieroglyphs... Imagine, my friend, what it is to see, lying in the sun, walking in the streets or mending shoes, men of consular type, each one a Cato or a Brutus, and not even lacking that haughty air which is appropriate to the masters of the world? Rome is no longer in Rome.' He contrasted the grace of the Arabs and their traditional ceremonies with the Parisians, pitiable 'in our corsets, tight shoes and ridiculous earrings' — a phrase which might seem to have prompted Baudelaire's contradictory plea, in his *Salon of 1845*, for a painter to show 'how grand we are in our frock-coats and leather boots'.

Delacroix probably needed time to digest the variety of his African experiences, for the works produced in the decade after this journey often have literary and medieval rather than Algerian subject matter. This is also explicable by the varied kinds of work which he was undertaking. He was beginning his great mural programme for the Palais Bourbon, discussed below, and although some Arab figures do appear in his decorative paintings, they were less suitable than classical and allegorical themes to furnish the dignity of a whole scheme. At this time, too, Delacroix began his sixteen lithographs for *Hamlet* published in 1843 and 1864, and the seven engravings (1836-43) devoted to Goethe's *Goetz von Berlichingen*.

One of the first works produced on his return, *The Rooms of Comte de Mornay*, shows even more documentary realism than we have observed in *Women of Algiers*. But in 1834 he also exhibited *Interior of a Dominican Convent in Madrid*, a scene of dark Rembrandtesque chiaroscuro inspired by a 'Gothic' tale *Melmoth the Wanderer* by the Englishman Charles Robert Maturin, and *The Battle of Nancy* which was probably painted before Delacroix went to Algeria. But other romantic works appeared after the African journey, including the somewhat cold-coloured *Prisoner of Chillon*, the lithograph of *Clifford Finding the Corpse of his Father on the Battlefield*, and at the end of the decade, *Hamlet and Horatio in the Graveyard*. It has been suggested that these were inspired by the early death of his nephew, Charles de Verninac, who was only two years younger than Delacroix.

Meanwhile a greater emphasis on order gradually emerged in both writings and paintings, accompanied perhaps by slightly less interest in force and conflict. Compositional order was imposed by the use of geometric frameworks, the severe and successful discipline of horizontals and verticals which may be seen in the *Chess Players in Jerusalem* (1835) and the *Jewish Wedding* of 1837-41 (plate 25) which is not only reminiscent of Classical and Renaissance pictures, but has been described by René Huyghe as 'a prelude to the geometrical construction of Mondrian'. The effect of the variegated gesturing crowd against the austere background is extremely powerful. Two pictures of Columbus (1838-9) are also based on a geometrical framework, and one, *The Return of Columbus from the New World* (plate 27) is reminiscent of Titian's *Presentation of the Virgin*, of which Delacroix had seen an engraving. Delacroix was not himself an expert in the use of linear perspective, but he is known to have taken advice from the famous scene painter Ciceri and his pupils, who drew in the architecture of *The Taking of Constantinople by the Crusaders*. As Lee Johnson observes, the influence of the theatre on Delacroix's painting has yet to be adequately studied.

Delacroix's large paintings of the late 30s and early 40s are generally constructed on a basis of great lines; as in *seicento* art, crossed diagonals often fill the surface and depth of the picture. Sometimes he achieves a contrapuntal effect and breaks the diagonal with the vertical lines of buildings or columns in the background, as in *The Justice of Trajan* (1840), a picture also indebted to French statues of the 17th century such as those by Puget. The principal group here forms a broad pyramid, supported against the central column. The theme of *The Justice of Trajan* is derived from an incident in Dante's *Purgatorio*, a book much admired in the early 19th century. In another great work of 1840, *The Taking of Constantinople by the Crusaders* (plate 32), Delacroix has contrived to give a very true rendering of real light and atmosphere. The colours are subtler and more muted than those in the *Trajan* — Baudelaire describes them as a stormy and lugubrious

harmony; he praises the swirling and billowing draperies and 'the emphatic truth of the gestures made by men at the great moments of life'. But neither the *Trajan* nor the *Crusaders* was well received by the critics in general, who took particular exception to Trajan's pink horse. The contrast in both these pictures between the stable architectural framework and the moving figures is intensified in *The Fanatics of Tangiers* (plate 26) based on an episode Delacroix had sketched on the spot in his note-book. Here the gesticulating and contorting Aissaovas painted with many red touches are set against the rectangular Arab houses, dazzling white or in shadow.

Some paintings of this time seem to be affected in their more sculptural treatment and new knowledge of anatomy, by the works which Delacroix was then doing on the walls of the Salon du Roi. In 1836 *Saint Sebastian Rescued by the Holy Woman* shows more solid volumes than usual; in composition it is derived from Rubens's *Deposition*. The *Medea* of 1838, one of Delacroix's classical masterpieces, began in a much more ferocious and abandoned form, according to the sketch, but in its final state (plate 31) was compact and symmetrical enough to win the admiration of Délécluze, veteran of Classicism and disciple of David. Its pyramidal composition probably owes something to Andrea del Sarto's *Charity* in the Louvre, which Delacroix admired and copied.

From about 1840 Delacroix's brush style became quicker and more free, his colours softer. He began to paint with small fluid touches, dividing his tones and sometimes interweaving the colours on a sketch already laid in, with grey and transparent tones. Strong contrasts of light gave way to blonde all-pervading atmosphere. Instead of working his brush strokes to a smooth finish, Delacroix now separated them. Sometimes he reserved oil for large surfaces, using watercolours for any smaller expanse; this gave him a more supple and nervous style. He was now painting far more rapidly, having prepared his way with great exactitude. All these changes found expression in his mural paintings, and may have been partly the result of the new techniques he needed for this work.

A considerable part of Delacroix's mature years was devoted to painting large mural decorations. He himself said that he was not made to create little things, and these commissions satisfied what he called 'the urge to create on a large scale which becomes overpowering once you have felt it'. In spite of his frail physique he was in many ways suited to this work. He had an exceptional gift for inventing forms, and an immense culture which enabled him to draw on a large stock of legends for his subject matter. Like his Venetian favourites, he was less interested in the detailed finish of an arm or leg than in the flowing unity of the whole. Few other painters since Poussin have had the power of giving so much clarity and meaning to a gesture. Hardly any of the themes chosen for murals were romantic or medieval, nor, as one would expect, did Delacroix make any attempt to portray modern heroism, although this was strongly advised by contemporary poets in the circle of Maxime du Champ, and was put in practice by Horace Vernet in his figure of a nude, presumably allegorical, engine-driver.

Delacroix's first large mural commission in 1833 to paint the Salon du Roi in the Palais Bourbon raised many difficulties, for unlike the great Venetians who often worked in rooms which they had themselves helped to design, Delacroix was confronted with dark surfaces punctuated by many doors, cupboards and niches. In this work, more than in those which followed, he was concerned with plasticity and sculptural effects, influenced by the contorted vigour of Michelangelo; some of the figures resemble the Moses and the judges in the Sistine Chapel. In 1837 Delacroix wrote a panegyric of Michelangelo in an article on Sigalon's copy of *The Last Judgement*. In 1838 he set up a school for training the assistants

he would need; the reminiscences of these pupils are often very detailed and enlightening about the procedure of the artist. According to one, Andrieu, Delacroix would often sit and contemplate his previous work all day without painting at all; at other times he would be seized with a fury and achieve a prodigious amount. He warned his assistants against too great an adherence to the model, which he felt would harm the idealized conception in the mind. (When Jean-Frédéric Bazille and Monet shared a studio above Delacroix's they were shocked to see that he often sent the model away before painting.) To choose a subject he would leaf through books of engravings, observing that Raphael had done the same.

For the Salon du Roi, Delacroix decided on friezes representing the living forces of the State — Industry, War, Justice, and so on, below which were grisaille allegorical figures representing the great French rivers. For the library of the same Palais Bourbon commissioned in 1838 he chose subjects which recall the general divisions of a library, for example Philosophy, Natural History, Theology, Literature, and Poetry. In the two half-domes he depicted the dawn and downfall of ancient civilization as epitomized by Orpheus bringing the arts of peace to primitive Greece, and Attila the Hun with his hordes over-running Italy and the Arts. The contrast between the restraint and calm of the Orpheus picture and the violent agitation of Attila has been achieved partly by a pronounced suppression of detail and broken brush-work, which gives an appearance of spontaneity to the latter.

Although Delacroix's murals may sound as if they were encyclopaedic in scope, they were in fact less comprehensive, intellectualised and dependent on subject matter than comparable work by contemporaries. The Utopian socialist Chenavard, commissioned in 1848 to paint the Panthéon, planned to represent the whole history of humanity, from the Creation to the French Revolution. and was only prevented by the withdrawal of his contract under the new Empire. At the height of his mural painting Delacroix could write in an article on Prud'hon: 'One finds a mysterious pleasure... and one having greater freedom from all impressions foreign to painting, in the contemplation of those scenes where subjects have no explanation; in them painting triumphs alone as music does in a symphony'. But of course it would have been impossible to carry out these large commissions without subject-matter, and Delacroix's themes were in fact poetically stimulating to him and fused successfully with their formal expression. Sometimes his pupils made suggestions to him; Villot claims to have been responsible for the programme in the Luxembourg Library which became an apotheosis of the great Greeks and Romans culminating in the presentation by Virgil of Dante to Homer.

Delacroix's choice for the ceiling of the Galerie d'Apollon in the Louvre was considerably limited by the need to harmonise it with the existing decorations of Le Brun, painted in the later part of the 17th century. In the event his *Triumph of Apollo* was one of his greatest tours de force. Gautier called him 'ce Le Brun flamboyante et romantique', and Odilon Redon later praised his 'couleur moral', observing that the painter has chosen each colour to suit the nature of the god depicted, so that, for example, Mars is a terrible violet, Venus a tender blue. The orchestration of this large ceiling is remarkable; unity is achieved not with the static balance of Raphael but by rivers of movement running diagonally through the whole. The subject, the precarious victory of the forces of light and civilization over the powers of darkness, runs through nearly all Delacroix's murals, and was so much a matter of faith with the painter that he was always ready to deride believers in progress and Utopia.

Delacroix's technical methods in the murals are well-documented by Louis de Planet, who recorded his master's instructions and advice. The need to achieve clear effects on badly lighted surfaces may be responsible for the progressive reduction of black and the use of white or very light underpainting to increase luminosity. Delacroix also gave very exact directions for producing naturalistic exchanges of coloured reflections. 'Everything in nature is reflection,' he declared, in opposition to Ingres, who maintained 'You must realise and never forget that reflection is no more than someone who is rather poor company'. In the murals Delacroix applied his ideas about variation in touch (in the size, shape and thickness of the brushstrokes) which he formulated in the entries to his journal intended as material for a 'Dictionary of the Fine Arts'. He managed to create an appearance of relief by emphasising the touch, and to give an illusion of receding planes by thin, smooth strokes. His agitated expressive use of the brush-stroke, as Lee Johnson observes, was developed further by Van Gogh, who greatly admired Delacroix.

Delacroix's last and probably his greatest mural paintings were the decorations in the Chapel of the Holy Angels at Saint Sulpice (1855-61). His subjects were *Heliodorus driven from the Temple*, a theme taken from one of Raphael's Vatican Stanze, and *Jacob Wrestling with the Angel* (plate 49), whose composition seems to have been inspired by Titian's altarpiece *The Death of St Peter Martyr* (Delacroix owned a copy of this work by Géricault.) The landscape of the *Jacob*, with its tall, heroic trees, makes a good contrast with the architectural setting of *Heliodorus*, where the lines all converge on the doomed man. Both angels have some resemblance to figures of Tintoretto; the avenging angel of the *Heliodorus* is particularly like the St Mark swooping down from the sky in the Accademia, Venice. (Stendhal considered Delacroix to be a disciple of Tintoretto.) These murals are characteristic of the later works in that nature and the human figures are seen as more interdependent.

Many of Delacroix's late pictures look back to his earlier themes, but there are some of a more pastoral kind treated with an almost Claude-like sense of magic and poetry; such are *Ovid among the Scythians*, *Angelica and the Wounded Medoro* and *Horses Emerging from the Sea*. Delacroix had felt an increasing love of nature since his visits to George Sand at Nohant in the 40s. These works are somewhat more loosely constructed than those like *The Jewish Wedding*, which as we have seen are set against geometrical backgrounds. Often they have a composition which ascends or moves in the form of an 'S' or zig-zag, as in *Arabs Skirmishing in the Mountains*, painted in the year of his death; at other times Delacroix returns to the Baroque diagonal which he had favoured less in the more geometrical and Classical period. Some new versions of old themes have the vehemence and wildness of his youth, notably the Berlin *Medea*, which is far less classical than the one of 1838 at Lille.

Delacroix, by precept and example, corrected the false idea of an inborn opposition between drawing and painting, an idea which had led to the belief that Titian, the greatest colourist, was a poor draughtsman. He realised also that there were two kinds of drawing; the first, depending on a rigorous contour-line, is retained in the picture as an independent structure, the second does not begin with the outline but from the masses in the centre, and it becomes merged in the pictorial units. Delacroix as a pupil of the Neo-Classicists began by admiring the first kind, and wrote in 1824: 'The first and most important thing in painting is outline.' But he soon discovered that in order to express energy and impatient force as he wished to do, the second kind as practised by Rubens, Titian and Correggio was more appropriate. Drawing was especially congenial to Delacroix because he valued rapidity of execution and the ability to express the essence of a composition in a few rapid strokes, neglecting what was less important: 'My precision would consist in

5 Portrait of Frédéric Villot. 1840.

21

strongly indicating only the principal objects, but in their relations to necessary action.' It is perhaps less surprising than it may have seemed to his executors that Delacroix, who during his lifetime kept his drawings hidden, left more than six thousand.

Delacroix, a man of complex intelligence and wide reading, constantly exercised his mind in writing. His journal and articles reflect the exploration of the self and of the nature of painting, his strivings and dissatisfaction. He is various and can pass readily from general speculation to some concrete particularity of colour, or the account of a visit to Chopin and George Sand. It is not surprising that in his articles he chose to discuss Raphael, Poussin and Michelangelo rather than his beloved Rubens, Veronese or Rembrandt. He needed to come to terms with art that was somewhat alien as a corrective to his own ferocity. As Valéry wrote, 'The theories of an artist always seduce him to love what he dislikes and to dislike what he really loves'. Certain themes recur constantly in Delacroix's writings — the rival claims of the fresh, spontaneous sketch and the finished picture, the need for solitude in spite of its melancholies, the dullness of realistic art. (There are similarly recurrent themes in the painting — two animals fighting or the lonely man of genius surrounded by fools and enemies.)

The 19th century was to see an art of colour and atmosphere with Delacroix as its prophet. Into the airless and discreetly tinted world of Neo-Classicism he brought the stormy colours of Rubens, the light open-air effects of Veronese. In Delacroix's work descriptive details were often blurred in the interests of a unity achieved less by outline than by colour and 'liaison' — 'that air, those reflections which form a whole of objects the most disparate in colour'. Delacroix had not the infallible tact of Corot in the juxtaposition of colours, and sometimes produced clichés and jarring effects, but he did not suffer from Corot's occasional insipidity. He valued

energy, conflict and force more than 18th century subtlety and grace. It was the movement and excitement in Delacroix which appealed to Cézanne and Van Gogh after the cool impersonality of the Impressionists. Van Gogh in Arles wrote that his art was fertilized by Delacroix rather than by the Impressionists. Yet Courbet, Manet and Degas copied *The Barque of Dante* as well as Cézanne and Gauguin.

It has been said of Delacroix that his pictures herald abstraction – the conquest of illustration by the play of chromatic forms – and it is true that he believed the mood and main theme of a picture should be recognisable by the colours from a distance before one could identify the actual subject. Nevertheless there are few artists, except Hogarth, who are further away from abstraction. Although he might have disliked the description Delacroix is, in fact, a literary painter; the stimulus of romantic plays and books was as important to him as the vision of an Algeria at once real yet ennobled by the antique grandeur which his school-books prepared him to recognise and acclaim.

SELECTED BOOK LIST

WELLINGTON, H.: *The Journal of Eugène Delacroix* (Phaidon Press 1951)

HUYGHE, RENÉ: *Delacroix* (Thames and Hudson 1963)

JOHNSON, LEE: *Delacroix* (Weidenfeld and Nicholson 1963)

SÉRULLAZ, MAURICE: *Les peintures murales de Delacroix* (Les Editions du Temps 1963)

Mémorial de l'Exposition Eugène Delacroix (Editions des Museés Nationaux 1963)

BAUDELAIRE, CHARLES: *The Painter of Modern Life and other Essays* (Phaidon Press 1964)
Art in Paris 1845-1862 Salons and other Exhibitions (Phaidon Press 1965)

Biographical outline

1798 April 26th. Ferdinand Victor Eugène Delacroix born at Charenton-Saint-Maurice on the outskirts of Paris, legally son of Charles Delacroix (1741-1805) a Minister under the Directoire and later a Prefect, and of Victoire Oeben (1758-1814), daughter of one of Louis XV's cabinet-makers. His real father was rumoured to be Talleyrand.

1806- Attends Lycée Impérial, Paris (later Lycée Louis-le-
1815 Grand). Wins awards for classics and drawing.

1814 After the death of his mother, the finances of the family decline.

1815 Lives with sister, Henriette de Verninac. Enters studio of Guérin at Ecole des Beaux-Arts, where he meets Géricault. Publishes first engravings and lithographs in *Le Miroir*.

1816 Copies after Old Masters in the Louvre.

1819 His first commission: *The Virgin of the Harvest*, for church at Orcemont, near Rambouillet.

1821 Géricault passes on to him a commission to paint *The Virgin of the Sacred Heart* for Ajaccio Cathedral. The actor Talma also commissions four panels of The Seasons for his dining-room.

1822 His first Salon exhibit, *The Barque of Dante*, causes a sensation. It is admired by Gros and Thiers and purchased by the State. In September begins his Journal.

1823 Moves into studio with English watercolourist, Thales Fielding. First reference in Journal to Constable.

1824 Copies Venetian masters. Affected by Géricault's death. Exhibits *The Massacre of Chios* at Salon. Discontinues Journal until 1847.

1825 May-August. Visit to England: meets Lawrence, Wilkie, Etty; sees performances of Shakespeare and Goethe's *Faust*. Begins liaison with Mme Dalton, which lasts about fifteen years.

1826 Associates with the Romantic circle, including Victor Hugo. First commission from State to paint *The Emperor Justinian composing his Laws*, now destroyed.

1827 Exhibits at Salon *The Death of Sardanapalus*; *The Execution of Doge Marino Faliero*.

1828 Publishes *Faust* lithographs.

1829 Publishes his first articles on art in the *Revue de Paris*; moves to the Quai Voltaire.

1831 Given the Légion d'Honneur by new government. Exhibits in Salon *Liberty Leading the People* and *The Murder of the Bishop of Liège*.

1832 In January accompanies Comte de Mornay on an embassy to the Sultan of Morocco. Visits Tangier, Meknes, Cadiz and Seville. Returns to France in July.

1833 Through Thiers, now Minister of Public Works, is commissioned to decorate the Salon du Roi, Palais Bourbon (completed December, 1837).

1834 Death of his nephew, Charles Verninac, a great shock. Stays at the home of his cousins in Valmont. *Women of Algiers* and *The Battle of Nancy* shown at Salon. Mme de Forget, his cousin, becomes his mistress.

1835 Beginning of ill-health, laryngitis, etc. Moves to the rue des Marais-Saint-Germain. Jenny le Guillou becomes his housekeeper, remaining until his death.

1837 Exhibits *The Battle of Taillebourg* at Salon.

1838 Commissioned to decorate the Library of the Chambre des Deputés, Palais Bourbon (finished December, 1847). Salon: *The Fanatics of Tangier* and *Medea*.

1839 Visits Belgium and Holland to see Rubens's works.

1840 *Pietà* for Saint-Denis du Saint-Sacrament commissioned (completed May, 1844). Commissioned to decorate the Library of the Senate, Palais du Luxembourg (completed December, 1846). Salon: *The Justice of Trajan*.

1841 Salon: *The Taking of Constantinople* and *Jewish Wedding in Morocco*.

1843 Publishes *Hamlet* lithographs.

1844 Rents house at Champrosay, near Fontainebleau and often stays there afterwards.

1845 Visits Pyrenees for treatment to his throat. Salon: *The Sultan of Morocco Surrounded by his Court*.

1846 Made an officer of the Légion d'Honneur. Salon: *The Abduction of Rebecca*.

1847 Resumes his Journal.

1848 Salon: *The Death of Lara; The Entombment*.

1849 Appointed to the Salon Hanging Committee and the Fine Arts Commission.

1850 Commissioned to decorate the Chapelle des Saints-Anges, St. Sulpice (completed July, 1861). Goes to Ems for cure, via Brussels, Antwerp, Cologne and Malines to see Rubens's work.

1851 Commissioned to decorate the ceiling of Salon de la Paix, Hôtel de Ville (completed March, 1854, destroyed by fire 1871).

1853 *Christ on the Sea of Galilee*.

1855 Thirty-five paintings shown at Exposition Universelle. Receives Grand Medaille d'Honneur and is made a Commander of the Légion d'Honneur.

1857 On eighth application elected to the Institute. Plans a 'Dictionary of the Fine Arts'. Moves to the Place Furstenberg.

1858 Salon: *View of Tangier from the Sea-shore; Death of Lara*.

1859 Exhibits at Salon for last time. *Ovid Among the Scythians. The Entombment*.

1861 Begins *The Four Seasons* for dining room of banker Hartmann.

1863 August 13th. Dies at the Place Furstenberg.

Delacroix on art

A writer has to say almost everything in order to make himself understood, but in painting it is as if some mysterious bridge were set up between the spirit of the persons in the picture and the beholder... Grosser minds are more easily moved by writers than by painters or musicians.

(Journal, 8th October, 1822)

What moves men of genius, or rather what inspires their work, is not new ideas, but their obsession with the idea that what has already been said is still not enough.

(Journal, 15th May, 1824)

We need to be very bold. Without daring, without extreme daring even, there is no beauty... We must therefore be almost beyond ourselves if we are to achieve all that we are capable of. (Journal, 21st July, 1850)

Man has in his soul innate sentiments which real objects will never satisfy and it is to these sentiments that the imagination of the painter and the poet is able to give form and life. Music, the first of the arts, what does it imitate?

(*Oeuvres Littéraires*, Vol. I.)

Painting does not always need a subject.

(Journal, 13th January, 1857)

Realism should be described as the Antipodes of art. It is perhaps even more detestable in painting and sculpture than in history and literature. (Journal, 22nd February, 1860)

Exactitude Exactitude is not art... The so-called conscientiousness of the majority of painters is only laborious perfection in the art of boring. (Journal, 18th July, 1850)

When Courbet painted the bottom of the woman bathing, he copied it scrupulously from a study which I saw beside his easel. Nothing is more cold; it is like inlaid woodwork... I did not begin to do anything passable on my African journey until the time when I had sufficiently forgotten the small details so as to recall in my pictures only the striking and poetical aspect; until then I was haunted by the love of exactitude which the majority take for truth.

(Journal, 17th October, 1853)

...the French defect of using line everywhere. And indeed this may be considered the greatest weakness of the French, compared with other schools. The slightest and most insignificant details are equally elaborated and are presented without any sacrifices or regard for the evil effect of such clumsy scrupulousness. (Journal, 29th October, 1857)

It is usually during a period of decadence that the greatest value is given to perfecting imitation.

(Supplement, Journal III.)

Pictorial Licence It is often to this that every master owes his most sublime effects; the unfinished condition in Rembrandt's work, the exaggeration in Rubens.

(Journal, 16th October, 1860)

Colour, shadow and reflections The law of green for the reflection and the edge of a shadow or a cast shadow, which I discovered earlier for linen, extends to everything, just as the three mixed (secondary) colours can be found in everything. I used to think that they were only present in certain objects. (*Oeuvres Littéraires*, Vol. I.)

Classicism I prefer to call Classical all regular works, those which satisfy the spirit not only by an exact, stately or striking way of painting objects and feelings, but still more by unity and logical order, in a word by all those qualities which increase the effect by means of simplicity.

(Journal, 13th January, 1857)

Titian and the Flemish painters catch the spirit of the Antique and are not mere imitators of its outward forms.

The Antique does not pay homage to charm, like Raphael and Correggio and the majority of the painters of the Renaissance. It has no affectation either of strength or the unexpected as in Michelangelo. It never sinks to the poor quality of parts of Puget's work, nor to his all-too-natural naturalness.

In the work of all these painters certain elements have become antiquated; there is nothing of this in the Antique. With the moderns there is always excess; in Antique art always the same moderation and the same sustained strength.

(Journal, 25th January, 1857)

... What characterizes the Antique is the expert amplitude of the forms combined with the feeling of life ... The true spirit of Antiquity does not consist in giving every isolated figure the appearance of a statue.

from the article on Prud'hon:
Revue des Deux-Mondes, 1st November, 1846)

It was reserved for our country to bring back in due course the taste for the simple and the beautiful. The works of the French philosophers reawakened a feeling for nature and the cult of Ancient Greece. David, in his painting, summarized the results of both.   (Journal, 9th October, 1862)

Poussin It seems that all his figures lack connection with each other and seem cut off; from this arise these gaps and this absence of unity, of depth and of effects which can be found in Le Sueur and all the colourists.

(Journal, 6th June, 1851)

'The Last Judgment' in the Sistine Chapel I can only perceive striking details, striking like a blow from the fist; but the interest, the unity, the captivation is absent from all this.   (Journal, 4th October, 1854)

Rembrandt Truly, it is only with Rembrandt that one can see the beginning in painting of that harmony of accessories with the principal subject which seems to me one of the most important, if not the most important, of its aspects. In Rembrandt, indeed — and this is perfection — the background and the figures make up a unity. The interest is everywhere; nothing can be divided up, just as in a beautiful view offered by nature where everything joins to enchant you.

(Journal, 29th July, 1854)

Rubens Admirable Rubens! What a magician! I grow angry with him at times; I quarrel with his heavy forms and his lack of refinement and elegance. But how superior he is to the collection of small qualities that make up the whole stock of other painters! ... Rubens did not correct himself and he was right ... I also note that his greatest quality (if you can imagine having to choose one quality in particular) is the astounding relief of his figures, that is to say their astonishing vitality.   (Journal, 21st October, 1860)

A hunt picture by Rubens Everything is done to strike the imagination and the execution is admirable. But the look of it is confused, the eye does not know where to fix itself, it has the feeling of wild disorder; it seems that art has not dominated enough to increase by careful arrangement or by sacrifices the effect of so many inventions of genius. His painting dominated by imagination is everywhere super-abundant; his accessories are too much elaborated; his picture is like a meeting where everyone is talking at the same time.

(Journal, 25th January, 1847)

Raphael One might say that his originality never seems more alive than in the ideas which he borrows. Everything which he finds he elevates and brings to life in a new way. It is he indeed who seems to be taking up what belongs to him and fertilizing seeds which were only awaiting his hand to yield their true fruits. (*Oeuvres Littéraires*, Vol. 2.)

No one can deny that with Raphael elegance takes precedence over naturalness, and that this elegance frequently degenerates into mannerism.

(Journal, 5th January, 1857)

Titian If we lived to be a hundred and twenty we should end by preferring Titian above everyone. He is not a young man's painter. He is the least mannered and consequently the most varied of artists.

. . . Titian originated that breadth of handling that broke sharply away from the dryness of his predecessors and is the very perfection of handling. Painters who deliberately cultivate this dryness of the Primitives . . . are like grown men imitating the speech and gestures of childhood in an attempt to appear ingenuous. (Journal, 5th January, 1857)

Those who see Titian simply as the greatest of the colourists make a grave error. He is that certainly, but at the same time he is the first of draughtsmen (if by drawing we understand drawing from nature and not that in which the artist's imagination plays a greater part than imitation).

(Journal, 25th January, 1857)

English Artists Lawrence, Turner and Reynolds and generally speaking all the great English painters have this defect of exaggeration, especially in the general effect, a fault that prevents their being ranked among the greatest masters. The cloudy and variable skies of their country lead them to produce these extravagant effects, these sudden contrasts of light and darkness, but they greatly exaggerate them, revealing defects caused by fashion or personal bias that speak louder than their fine qualities.

(Journal, 8th February, 1860)

Edgar Allan Poe When I came home I continued my reading of Edgar Allan Poe. His work revives that sense of the Mysterious which I used to be so much concerned with in my painting and which I threw off, I believe, by working in situ on allegorical subjects. Baudelaire says in his preface that my painting reminds him of Poe's feeling for a strange ideal that finds enjoyment in the terrible. He is quite right, but the incoherence and obscurity that Poe mingles with his conceptions do not suit my ideas.

(Journal, 30th May, 1856)

BAUDELAIRE ON DELACROIX

What is this strange mysterious quality which Delacroix, to the glory of our age, has interpreted better than anyone else? It is the invisible, the impalpable, the dream, the nerves, the soul . . . Eugène Delacroix, at the same time as being a painter in love with his craft, was a man of general education as opposed to the other artists of today, who for the most part are little more than illustrious or obscure daubers — mere artisans, possessing some the ability to manufacture academic figures, others fruit and others cattle. Eugène Delacroix loved and had the ability to paint *everything*, and knew also how to appreciate every kind of talent . . . The most manifest characteristic of Delacroix's style is its concision and a kind of unobtrusive intensity — the customary result of a concentration of the entire mental powers upon a given point . . . Delacroix had a very marked sympathy for concise and concentrated writers – for writers whose simple and unadorned prose seems to imitate the swift movements of thought and whose sentences are like gestures — Montesquieu for example. Eugène Delacroix was a curious mixture of scepticism, politeness, dandyism, burning determination, craftiness, despotism and finally of a sort of personal kindness and tempered warmth which always accompanies genius. Eugène Delacroix never lost the traces of his Revolutionary origin. It may be said of him, as of Stendhal, that he had a great dread of being made a fool of. Sceptical and aristocratic, he only knew passion and the supernatural through his forced intimacy with the world of dreams. A hater of the masses, he really only thought of them as iconoclasts, and the acts of violence perpetrated upon several of his works in 1848 were ill-suited to convert him to the political sentimentalism of our times.

There was much of the savage in Eugène Delacroix — this was in fact the most precious part of his soul, the part which was entirely dedicated to the painting of his dreams and to the worship of his art. There was also much of the man of the world; that part was destined to disguise and excuse the other . . . You might have called him a volcanic crater artistically concealed behind bouquets of flowers. Another feature of resemblance with Stendhal was his propensity for simple formulas, brief maxims for the proper conduct of life.

The morality of his works — if it is at all permissible to speak of ethics in painting — is also visibly marked with Molochism. His works contain nothing but devastation, massacres, conflagrations; everything bears witness against the eternal and incorrigible barbarity of man.

from 'The Life and Work of Eugène Delacroix' by Charles Baudelaire (1863) translated and edited by Jonathan Mayne in *The Painter of Modern Life and other essays.*

Notes on the illustrations

BLACK AND WHITE ILLUSTRATIONS

Figure 2 *Study for The Moroccan Blacksmith*. 1853. Black lead, squared for transfer with white chalk 6½ × 10⅜ in. (16.3 × 26.3 cm.). Musée du Louvre, Paris.

This is the final study for the painting Delacroix described as 'the man shoeing his horse', which has double and discontinuous contour lines, probably not because it was unfinished but as an experiment in the relationship of light, form and atmosphere. This, as Lee Johnson says, anticipates Cézanne. The light, shimmering touch produces an atmospheric rather than a hard linear effect. George Sand in her *Impressions et Souvenirs* records that Delacroix would say: 'Neither the light which strikes an outline nor the shadow which glides under it has any discernible boundary'.

Figure 3 *Delacroix and his Friends on New Year's Eve*. 1817. Indian ink wash and pencil. 10 × 8 in. (25 × 22 cm.). Cabinet des Dessins, Musée du Louvre, Paris.

In early life, before Delacroix used much watercolour, he discovered that wash suited his painting style and that he could employ it as here for the simple contrasts of value. This sketch illustrates the importance in Delacroix's life of his men friends, of whom he was particularly fond. These were a heterogeneous company, including Chopin, Chenavard, Bonington, Le Comte de Mornay, and Villot.

Figure 4 *Two Seated Moors in Conversation*. 1832. Pen and ink over pencil. 7¼ × 11⅛ in. (19.2 × 28.3 cm.). Clark Institute (Inventory 1414 Reg. No. 1211) Williamstown, Mass.

This very different drawing is both skilful and highly-finished, unlike much of Delacroix's work, which was left in an apparently sketchy state in order to preserve the spontaneity, and was often criticized by contemporaries on this score. It formed part of a sketch–book used in Morocco which has now been broken up.

Figure 5 *Portrait of Frédéric Villot*. c. 1840. Black chalk and pencil. 13⅛ × 9⅜ ins. (33.3 × 23.7 cm.). Fogg Museum, Cambridge, Mass.

Villot was one of Delacroix's oldest friends; this drawing probably dates from about eight or ten years after the painted portrait. Delacroix perhaps slightly preferred the company of Villot's wife Pauline, but he was also fond of Frédéric. Villot became a disastrous curator of the Louvre; the restorations, often carried out by himself, aroused such violent criticism that in 1860 he was forced to resign his post as Curator of Paintings. Delacroix wrote in the journal that Villot has 'destroyed a Veronese with his attentions'.

THE COLOUR PLATES

All paintings are oil on canvas unless otherwise stated

Plate 1 *Portrait of Elizabeth Salter*. c. 1818. Oil on paper laid down on canvas. 9⅝ × 7½ in. (24 × 19 cm.). Collection of Le Comte Doria, Paris.

This portrait is presumed to be of Elizabeth Salter, an English girl in the service of Delacroix's sister. Delacroix fell in love with her and wrote her letters in very bad English. 'O my lips are arid since had been cooled so deliciously . . . You are a cruel person which play afflicting the anothers.' The sharp contours and smooth modelling here resemble the portraits of Ingres, and Delacroix was probably alluding to this work when in April, 1824, writing of the incisive contour of Ingres, he added 'There is something of it in my Salter.'

Plate 2 *Seated Nude, Figure Study, Mademoiselle Rose*. c. 1821-23. 31⅞ × 25½ in (81 × 65 cm.). Musée du Louvre, Paris.

Delacroix painted two academic studies of Mlle Rose, a favourite model. The turn of the neck, the sculptural and frontal treatment, the colour scheme—all seem more indebted to David even than to Guérin, his pupil and Delacroix's teacher. The Classical bent of Delacroix's art at the beginning of his career is mirrored in his letters, which express admiration for Virgil, Chenier and Poussin.

Plate 3 *Self-Portrait as Ravenswood. c.* 1824. 16 ⅛ × 12 ¾ in. (40.9 × 32.3 cm.). Musée du Louvre, Paris.
French artists of the Romantic generation enjoyed portraying themselves in fancy dress. Delacroix had ample opportunity for studying the bold technique of Spanish painting in the collections plundered during the Napoleonic wars. He greatly admired Velasquez and copied a picture of this master's pupil Carreño da Miranda; the copy is similar in style to this self-portrait. Even before the visit to London in 1825 Delacroix had been inspired by themes from the novels of Walter Scott, and this continued until late in life (see *The Abduction of Rebecca* below). Ravenswood is the hero of Scott's *Bride of Lammermoor*. But the inscription Ravenswood on the back of the canvas may only refer to Delacroix's nickname for the recipient.

Plate 4 *Head of a Woman. c.* 1820. 17 × 12 ¼ in. (43 × 31 cm.). Collection M. Leonardo Benatov, Paris.
This is one of Delacroix's early works which appears to be influenced by Géricault in its vigorous handling and sombre colours. Sérullaz has suggested that it is connected with the *Virgin of the Sacred Heart* (plate 5). Less plausibly it has been considered a study for the other church-piece of this time, the Raphaelesque *Virgin of the Harvest* at Orcement.

Plate 5 *The Virgin of the Sacred Heart.* 1821. 101 ⅝ × 60 in. (258 × 152 cm.). Ajaccio Cathedral.
This work was originally commissioned from Géricault by M. de Forbin, Directeur des Musées, but this painter did not find the theme inspiring, and asked Delacroix to paint it under his name. It was originally destined for Nantes, but apparently went to Ajaccio instead in 1827. Letters to Delacroix's sister show that he too was finding the project difficult, partly perhaps because he was distracted by unfulfilled plans for visiting Italy and by his picture for the next Salon *The Barque of Dante*. It is a less Raphaelesque work, more sculptural than his previous *Virgin of the Harvest* at Orcement, which had been his first commissioned work.

Plate 6 *The Barque of Dante.* 1822. 74 ½ × 96 ⅞ in. (18.9 × 24.6 cm.). Musée du Louvre, Paris.
Delacroix's first Salon picture shows the shades of the damned clinging to the boat in which Dante and Virgil are being ferried across the lake surrounding the infernal city of Dis. Delacroix apparently told his favourite pupil Andrieu that nearly all the figures had been sketched from the same male model, but several of the poses derive from Michelangelo and Rubens, and the boatman Phlegyas is based on the Hellenistic Belvedere torso. In addition to a debt to Géricault in choice of subject-matter and colour, Lee Johnson has suggested that Géricault's drawings, executed in Italy, rather than engravings of Michelangelo, are likely to have been a source. The theme of beings whether human or animal, at the mercy of destruction, is a recurrent one in Delacroix's art. This picture won the immediate praise of Gros and Thiers.

Plate 7 *The Natchez.* 1823?-1835. 35 ½ × 45 ¾ in. (90 × 116 cm.). Lord and Lady Walston, Cambridgeshire.
This is a typically Romantic subject, the only theme which Delacroix took from Chateaubriand. In the novel *Atala*, published in 1801, the hero Rene's granddaughter has given birth to a child after she and her husband had fled from the French who are destroying his Red Indian tribe. It was characteristic of the Primitivism of the time to make heroes

of 'children of nature' and to enjoy scenes set in lonely country away from civilisation. The figures are amongst the best in Delacroix's early art and the position of the mother with the child was carefully worked out in a preliminary chalk drawing. Although most of the picture was probably executed in the early 1820s, there may have been some re-working before it was first shown in the Salon of 1835.

Plate 8 *The Massacre of Chios*. 1824. 164×139 in. (417× 354 cm.). Musée du Louvre, Paris.
This massacre of Greeks by Turks took place in April, 1822 and by May, 1823 Delacroix was noting in his diary that he had decided to take it as his subject for a Salon picture. A French officer serving with the Greeks, Colonel Voutier, reported the facts in his *Mémoires*, and Delacroix, through his brother-in-law Raymond de Verninac, was able to meet him. (This self-documentation by Delacroix was not habitual.) He also borrowed oriental costumes from his friend Auguste. The stages of painting are more thoroughly recorded than for any other work by Delacroix. Although he did lighten his palette and use small touches of vibrant paint as a result of admiring works by Constable, there is some doubt whether he made these changes at the last minute as Villot reported. The reception of this work was on the whole unfavourable. Gros called it a massacre of painting, and Stendhal said it had the same sad kind of exaggeration as the poetry of de Vigny, but he conceded that the figures had merit. The picture was bought by the state and Delacroix obtained a second class medal. Many studies exist for it in different media.

Plate 9 *The Penance of Jane Shore*. 1824. 10⅝×8¼ in. (27×21 cm.). Collection Dr W. F. Schnyder, Solothurn, Switzerland.
This English subject was also treated by Blake and some of his early Romantic contemporaries. Jane Shore, the wife of a London merchant, had become the mistress of Edward IV, but on his death was condemned for witchcraft by Richard III and made to wander about the streets starving and holding a lighted taper. Delacroix has chosen to show the moment when her husband vainly attempts to help her. There were performances of two different plays on this theme in Paris in 1824. Delacroix may have been inspired by one of these or by a French translation of Nicholas Rowe's tragedy (1713). He also did at least one lithograph of the same subject.

Plate 10 *Study for Baron Schwiter*. 1826. 21¾×17⅞ in. (55× 45 cm.). Springfield Museum of Fine Arts, Massachusetts.
This bust study for the portrait of Baron Schwiter is far more impetuous and full of brio than the somewhat languid aristocrat of the final picture. It bears a faint resemblance to some portraits of the young Napoleon. Like the final work, it seems influenced by Sir Thomas Lawrence.

Plate 11 *Portrait of Baron Schwiter*. 1826?-30. 85¾×56½ in. (218×143.5 cm.). National Gallery, London.
Louis-Auguste Schwiter (1805-89) was a painter and friend of Delacroix. The stance and 'the noble air and distinguished manner — the most delicate shade of melancholy . . .' in the features of the sitter may owe something to Sir Thomas Lawrence, whom Delacroix praised for these qualities. Lawrence often painted a dandy or aristocrat against the background of a park as here. Moreau, who knew Delacroix, says that the picture was refused at the Salon of 1827 and that the landscape was partly painted by Paul Huet.

Plate 12 *The Execution of the Doge Marino Faliero*. 57×45 in. (145×115 cm.). Wallace Collection, London.
This was painted soon after Delacroix's return from England at a time when he was seeing a great deal of Bonington, whose influence is here noticeable, partly in the bright,

rather glossy colours. It is particularly like Bonington's *Palace of the Doges* (1826), now in the National Gallery of Canada. The subject is taken from a play by Byron written in 1820. The picture was shown at the Salon of 1827-8 with this explanation: 'The Doge Marino Faliero, having conspired against the Republic, is condemned to be beheaded on the stairs of the Doge's palace at Venice. After the execution, one of the members of the Council of Ten holds the bleeding sword aloft in the air to show the people, saying "Justice punished the traitor".' The Louvre owns a number of sketches for this composition in water-colour, pen and Indian ink.

Plate 13 *The Death of Sardanapalus*. 1827. 145 × 195 in. (395 × 495 cm.). Musée du Louvre, Paris.
This work, intended for the Salon of 1827 but not ready in time, was fiercely criticised in the Salon of 1828 as 'confused', 'imitating Rubens without his talent for design', 'romantic' and 'ridiculous'. Thoré and a few others praised 'the fresh, flower-like colouring', which owes something to the fluidity of English water-colours. The subject has generally been thought to derive from Byron's play *Sardanapalus*, published in 1821, but neither in Byron nor in the Classical sources used by him is there any mention of the massacre of the king's concubines. Either this addition derives from what Baudelaire called Delacroix's 'Molochism' — his love of pain and bloodshed — or, as Lee Johnson has suggested, it was taken from certain engravings of ancient Etruscan art by A.F. Gore. This is probably the first major work of Delacroix to make use of the Baroque diagonal composition. There are a great number of studies for this work, in chalk, pen, pastel and sanguine, and a large, vehement and successful oil-study.

Plate 14 *Greece Expiring on the Ruins of Missolonghi*. 1827. 82 ½ × 58 in. (209 × 147 cm.). Musée des Beaux-Arts, Bordeaux.

This was the third theme for the Greek war against the Turks painted by Delacroix. Missolonghi was beseiged in 1822, 1823 and 1825; on the last occasion the inhabitants found it impossible to resist and fled leaving nothing but ruins. Delacroix would of course associate the name with the death of his hero Byron in 1824. The allegorical figure looks somewhat like the personification of Liberty (plate 16) but the model was probably the same as for *The Woman with a Parrot*. In this picture there is a fine rendering of a hand in the manner perhaps of Géricault. *Greece Expiring* was first shown in London, but it was bought by the City of Bordeaux, which greatly pleased Delacroix, who had lived there once.

Plate 15 *Woman with a Parrot*. 1827. 10 × 15 in. (25 × 39 cm.). Musée des Beaux-Arts, Lyons.
During the period immediately following his return from England, Delacroix painted several odalisques (female slaves, popular as a subject with Ingres and others). This, the best known, seems to be influenced by Bonington (and perhaps other English artists such as Etty) in its fluid handling and use of red and gold. There is a chalk study for the model with less draping. One wonders how far it was the inspiration for Courbet's work of similar subject and very different handling.

Plate 16 *Liberty Leading the People*. 1830. 102 × 128 in. (260 × 325 cm.). Musée du Louvre, Paris.
Of this well-known work inspired by the July Revolution in Paris, Delacroix wrote to his brother: 'I have undertaken a modern subject, a scene on the barricades... and if I haven't fought for my country at least I have painted for her.' (Delacroix's brother was a general.) There are a great many pencil studies of houses and figures for this work. Writers have wished to identify Delacroix himself with the militant figure in a top hat, but Dumas, in a lecture given

in 1864, said that Delacroix did not take part in the fighting. Others have said that it was Frédéric Villot, future curator of the Louvre, and a friend of Delacroix. The young boy brandishing a pistol may have later suggested Victor Hugo's character Gavroche in *Les Misérables*. On the whole Delacroix was praised for this picture, which was bought by the new government, but the critic of *Le Moniteur des Arts* said that it would be difficult to imagine Delacroix's Liberty as a more hideous woman if he had been intending to represent Licence!

Plate 17 *Boissy d'Anglas at the Convention*. 1831. 31 × 41 in. (79 × 104 cm.). Musée des Beaux-Arts, Bordeaux.
Boissy d'Anglas (1756-1826) was in the chair at a session of the National Convention in 1795 when a mob broke in and began to threaten him. A young deputy, Féraud, was shot trying to protect him, and his head on a pile was shown to the chairman, but Boissy d'Anglas kept his sangfroid for hours until the mob was finally routed by reinforcements. Delacroix was a school friend of the President of the Convention's son and admired the former. This subject, with others including *Mirabeau and Dreux-Brézé*, was set soon after the Revolution of 1830, in a competition for decorating the hall where the sessions were held in the Palais-Bourbon. Delacroix produced canvases for both these subjects, but won neither of the prizes, which went to the now unknown painters Vinchon and Court. There was some indignation in the press about this. This is one of the dark, shadowy pictures surging with figures which may be influenced by Delacroix's new interest in Rembrandt and lithograph technique, at about this time.

Plate 18 *The Battle of Nancy*. 1831. 94⅛ × 141⅜ in. (239 × 359 cm.). Musée des Beaux-Arts, Nancy.
Delacroix was commissioned to paint this subject by Charles X after a visit he made to the military hospital at Nancy in 1828. It has been suggested by Thérèse Charpentier that the picture may have been intended to have some propaganda value, since the Duke of Lorraine could represent legitimate rule and Charles the Bold could stand for defeated ambition (like Napoleon's). The exact moment of the battle to be depicted, the stumbling and death of Charles the Bold, was discussed and decided upon in detail by the King, the city officials, the Minister of the Interior and the painter. The picture was completed before the Moroccan journey, but not exhibited at the Salon until 1834. Later there were complaints that Delacroix had been historically inaccurate, but we know from letters that he did try to document himself, and Lee Johnson suggests that in major respects Delacroix was more correct about the battle than his critics. The triangular arrangement in depth of the foreground figures has been compared with those of Gros in *Napoleon on the Battlefield at Eylau*. Degas copied this picture and the treatment of landscape may have influenced his *War in the Middle Ages* (1865).

Plate 19 *A Street in Meknes*. 1832 .18¼ × 25⅜ in. (46.3 × 64.5 cm.). Albright-Knox Art Gallery, Buffalo, New York.
This picture, exhibited in the 1834 Salon, was the first of Delacroix's North African subjects to be shown there; it was rather naturally eclipsed by the *Women of Algiers* and considered by the critics as natural but somewhat slight and sketch-like. Meknes was the destination of the French mission, but Mornay and his companions were not allowed to move about the town for another week and then the few who, like Delacroix, wished to do so, had to pay for soldiers to escort them. It was from Meknes that he wrote: 'The picturesque abounds here. At every step there are ready-made pictures that would ensure the fortune and glory of twenty generations of painters.' This is perhaps his first picture to show human figures rather carefully aligned against the geometrical shapes of white walls.

Plate 20 *Women of Algiers*. 1834. 71×90¼ in. (180×229 cm.). Musée du Louvre, Paris.

This is one of Delacroix's finest pictures and one of the few with a peaceful subject and not one of conflict or bloodshed. Towards the end of his visit Delacroix was admitted to the somewhat rare spectacle of Mohammedan women in the intimacy of their own apartments. There are at least thirteen studies for this work made from nature in chalk and water-colour, besides seven others, some in oil, executed in the studio. Charles Cournault, a friend of Delacroix's and Director of the Nancy Museum, relates that when speaking afterwards of this visit, Delacroix became excited and cried: 'It's beautiful! It's as it was in the time of Homer! The woman in the gynæceum, concerning herself with her children and embroidering wonderful clothes, that is woman as I understand her!' Delacroix in this work struck a very successful balance between the naturalism of the colours (see page 15) and the needs of decorative harmony. However, the critic of *Le Constitutionnel* declared that all five of Delacroix's pictures in this Salon were marked by 'negligence and too much facility', lamenting that the mural commissions had been given to such a painter. A second large version, varying considerably in the distribution of figures and light, was shown at the Salon of 1849. Amongst the most well-known admirers who have based work on the *Women of Algiers* are Renoir and Picasso.

Plate 21 *Portrait of Madame Simon*. 1834. 23½×19¼ in. (59.7×48.9 cm.). City Museum and Art Gallery, Birmingham.

This is Delacroix's only surviving portrait in oils where the sitter is placed in a fully described setting, and in this and the casual pose almost anticipates Degas's early portraits (cf. *The Bellili family*). Delacroix also painted a bust-length portrait of Mme Simon, who was the wife of the balletmaster

at the Paris Opéra. This is a more Davidian, more smoothly painted work than many of the paintings contemporary with it.

Plate 22 *Hamlet and Horatio in the Graveyard*. 1839. 32½×26 in. (82×66 cm.). Musée du Louvre, Paris.

Like many of the Romantics, Delacroix could probably identify himself with the character of Hamlet. He must have read this play in translation by 1817, when he signed himself 'Yorick' in a letter. There are at least four versions of this theme; the earliest (dated 1835) does not include the grave-diggers with Yorick's skull. It is a much more open composition, and the setting is believed to be reminiscent of a cemetery overlooked by Delacroix during the time he was kept in quarantine at Toulon on his return from Africa.

Plate 23 *Self-Portrait*. c. 1835-7. 26×21 in. (65×54 cm.). Musée du Louvre, Paris.

This, the most characteristic and well-known of the self-portraits, was kept by Delacroix and left in his will to his devoted housekeeper Jenny Le Guillou, who bequeathed it to the Louvre in 1872. It is sufficiently like another and unfinished self-portrait in darker colours to convince one that it resembled the sitter.

Plate 24 *Moroccan Caid Visiting a Tribe*. 1837. 38½×50 in. (98×126 cm.). Musée des Beaux-Arts, Nantes.

This picture, like the very different *Sultan of Morocco Surrounded by his Court* (plate 36), was based on a scene which Delacroix had witnessed, in this case at Alcassar-el-Kebir, in 1832, and drawn in his note-book. He several times depicted the gesture of a rider reining in his horse. This version seems less composed than others and has the more naturalistic, documentary treatment of shadows and colour which we find in the *Women of Algiers*.

Plate 25 *Jewish Wedding in Morocco.* 1837-41. 41 ⅜ × 55 ¼ in. (105 × 140 cm.). Musée du Louvre, Paris.

This, one of Delacroix's most celebrated works, was commissioned by Comte Maison, who then refused it, disliking both picture and price. Delacroix stayed over a month at Tangier, and became friendly with a Jew, Abraham-ben-Chimol, who allowed the painter to draw his family. In the note-books there are two studies in water-colour and a long, detailed description of the wedding ceremony, which he also published in the *Magasin Pittoresque* of January, 1842. In a letter he praised the Jews for retaining so much more of the grace inherent in their old customs than did the contemporary French. 'True grace is superior to knowledge' he said. The geometrical, almost classical, composition of this work even won the approval of the Davidian Délécluze when it was shown at the Salon of 1841.

Plate 26 *The Fanatics of Tangier.* 1836-8. 39 ½ × 52 ½ in. (98 × 131 cm.). Jerome Hill Collection, New York.

Another example of the relationship between semi-geometrical architecture and human beings in violent movement. The picture is almost certainly based again on incidents seen by Delacroix on the African journey, although there are no references to them in the correspondence or notes. Some of the more contorted figures were roughly sketched in a wash drawing which could have been done on the spot, and the theme occurs also in a series of eighteen water-colours painted for Comte de Mornay. The fanatics were Aissaovas, disciples of Sidi-Mohammed-Ibn-Aissa, who had founded the sect about three centuries earlier. Delacroix explained, when the picture was exhibited at the Salon of 1838, that 'they get into a truly drunken state, then, spreading into the streets, they abandon themselves to a thousand contortions and often commit dangerous acts.' In 1857 Delacroix made a much smaller variant of this theme, in which far greater stress is

laid on individual fanatics, and the sharp geometrical volumes of the houses has become vaguer and more atmospheric. This abandonment of comparatively tight architectural framework for the figures is characteristic of the later style. In 1838 Gustave Planche admired it from a distance, but liked it less near to, but Gautier praised its authenticity from personal experience of the fanatics.

Plate 27 *The Return of Columbus from the New World.* 1839. 33 ½ × 45 ½ in. (85 × 115.6 cm.). Toledo Museum of Art, U.S.A.

Another example, from these years, of a picture composed with a severe framework of verticals and horizontals, in this case based on Titian's well-known *Presentation of the Virgin in the Temple* in the Accademia at Venice; Delacroix would almost certainly have known an engraving of the latter. Two pictures were commissioned on the life of Columbus for the Palace of San Donato, Florence; the other one shows an incident before the voyage when Columbus and his son, as dusty travellers, were befriended by the Prior of the Franciscan monastery of La Rabida. The two pictures, of the same size, were no doubt intended as pendants, and the scene in the monastery is also worked out on carefully chosen geometrical lines. Bracquemond, friend of Manet and Degas, made an engraving of this picture for the sale of the San Donato pictures in 1870.

Plate 28 *Portrait of George Sand.* 1838. 31 × 22 ½ in. (79 × 57 cm.). Ordrupgaard Museum, Copenhagen.

Delacroix did not know George Sand until comparatively late in her life, after she had broken with Alfred de Musset. François Buloz, the editor of the *Revue des Deux Mondes*, wishing to show his readers the portraits of his principal contributors, commissioned Delacroix to paint her. This picture, showing George Sand with short hair and sunken eyes, is in a private collection, and was later engraved. It led to a friendship between the novelist and painter, who, towards the beginning of George Sand's liaison with Chopin, probably in the summer or autumn of 1838, began to paint a double portrait of the two lovers. Already in 1873 the works was separated into two parts (see No. 29), but one can see from a pencil drawing what Delacroix's original conception was like. It has been suggested that George Sand's son Maurice, who disliked Chopin, had the two portraits separated, or that it was done for financial reasons. It is possible that this portrait was unfinished and that Delacroix was working towards the more sculptural effect shown in his *Cleopatra* and *The Sybil* painted about the same time.

Plate 29 *Portrait of Frédéric Chopin.* 1838. 18 ⅛ × 14 ⅞ in. (45 × 38 cm.). Musée du Louvre, Paris.
Delacroix knew Chopin considerably before the latter knew George Sand. They liked each other and Delacroix appreciated Chopin's power as composer and pianist, but the latter did not care for the 'new tendencies' in Delacroix's painting. In the study for the double portrait (see No. 28) Chopin was to be shown at the piano, and in September 1838 Delacroix wrote to his friend Pierret, asking him to get the same piano delivered as Chopin had previously borrowed. There are at least two other drawings of Chopin by Delacroix. The brush-work in this portrait is loose and undefined, but this may be deliberate.

Plate 30 *The Shipwreck of Don Juan.* 1840. 53 × 77 in. (135 × 196 cm.). Musée du Louvre, Paris.
This picture, exhibited in the Salon of 1841, took its theme from Byron's poem *Don Juan*, Canto 2, Stanza 75; it shows the moment when lots were being drawn for a victim and the lot fell on Don Juan's tutor.
The picture is painted in thick impasto and, as Baudelaire

wrote, 'the low, heavy sky weighs down like a lid.' The boat had been a recurring theme in Delacroix's work ever since he saw *The Raft of the Medusa*, and he must certainly have been aware of its symbolism as a way of expressing the passage across life. He had copied in his journal Michelangelo's metaphor in which the course of his life becomes a frail bark in a stormy sea. There are numerous studies for this picture, including one in oil in the Victoria and Albert Museum, London, and a picture apparently painted about seven years later, showing castaways in a boat where two are throwing a third, dead or alive, overboard. In 1853 the subject was replaced by *Christ on the Sea of Galilee*, (plate 43) which clearly has a more hopeful outcome than Don Juan's boat tossed in a deserted sea.

Plate 31 *Medea About to Kill her Children.* 1838. 102 ⅜ × 65 in. (260 × 164 cm.). Musée des Beaux Arts, Lille.
This subject had interested Delacroix since 1824, and continued to do so until the end of his life. His original studies had been more stormy and full of movement, but he gradually reduced them to this more sculptural composition, which is almost Raphaelesque in the careful juxtaposition of bodies, though not in the convulsive posture. Another version, of 1859, now in the Berlin Gallery, is more expressionist and turbulent in mood. Delacroix seems to have been satisfied with this prototype, since he alluded to it in his candidature for the Academy, along with *The Barque of Dante, The Massacre at Chios, The Justice of Trajan*, and *The Entry of the Crusaders into Constantinople*. Even the classical Délécluze praised it, though few admired the drawing of the half-shadow across Medea's face. Medea is about to murder her children by Jason in revenge, because Jason has deserted her for Glauce, daughter of the King of Corinth. Delacroix was more probably inspired here by Corneille than by Euripides.

Plate 32 *The Taking of Constantinople by the Crusaders, 1204.* 1840. 161⅜ × 196 in. (410 × 498 cm.). Musée du Louvre, Paris.

This work was commissioned in 1838 by Louis-Philippe for the gallery of historical pictures in the Pavillon du Roi in the Louvre. The incident took place in the Fourth Crusade set on foot by Innocent III to free Jerusalem from the Muslims, after the Crusaders, diverted by intrigues to Constantinople, had taken the city. The picture does not show the assault on the city, but the subsequent procession through the streets, led by Baudouin Count of Flanders, whom the inhabitants are imploring for mercy. There are numerous preparatory drawings for this work; one published for the first time by Lee Johnson has a faint colour circle with the names of the primary colours and their complementaries on the circumference and a line connecting each primary with its complementary. Chevreul's book *Of the law of the simultaneous contrast of Colours and the Assortment of coloured objects* was published in 1839, but Delacroix could have known about these discoveries from lectures or conversations. He also derived much of this subtlety of colours from studying Old Masters such as Veronese, who also allowed daylight and colours to penetrate his shadows. The colour harmonies in the *Crusaders* are colder and more subdued than those of *The Justice of Trajan*, so that the picture has been described as expressing exhaustion. *Le Constitutionnel* spoke of 'the confused and strangled composition, the dull earthy colours and the lack of definite contours', but Baudelaire praised the 'abstraction faite'.

Plate 33 *The Bride of Abydos.* 1843. 22 × 17¾ in. (56 × 45 cm.). Musée du Louvre, Paris.

Delacroix first read *The Bride of Abydos* in 1824 and mentioned Selim's death as one of the passages of Byron to re-read in order to inspire himself. In several pictures he showed Lara endeavouring to restrain Selim from signalling to his men, but in this, the small version in the Louvre, he is preparing to defend his bride. The two figures are set against one of those rocky sea-scapes beloved by Delacroix in his later years. The sword curving round her head anchors the composition in a way perhaps reminiscent of Poussin's fluttering scarf in *The Triumph of Neptune*. Mr George Heard Hamilton has pointed out that Delacroix was probably influenced here by the English illustrators of Byron, particularly Stothard, who treated this theme in an engraving.

Plate 34 *Orpheus Bringing the Arts of Peace to the Primitive Greeks.* 1843-7. Oil and wax on plaster. 289 × 434 in. (735 × 1100 cm.). Half-dome, Library of Palais-Bourbon.

Delacroix was always keenly aware that civilisation rested on thin foundations and is perpetually menaced by destruction. In the library of the Palais-Bourbon he embodied the battle between the two forces, showing on one of the half-domes Orpheus bringing the arts of peace, or the dawn of civilisation, in a calm, idyllic scene and finished technique, on the other Attila's swift and devastating advance, painted more impressionistically, with daring suppression of details. The *Orpheus* is probably one of the ancestors of other 19th century idylls set in Antiquity, such as those of Puvis de Chavannes and Degas's Spartiates. The Nymph rising from the bulrushes derives from a figure of Spring in Delacroix's decorations for the actor Talma's dining-room, and thence from a crouching Aphrodite in a Greco-Roman wall-painting.

Plate 35 *The Death of Ophelia.* 1844. 9 × 12 in. (22 × 30 cm.). Musée du Louvre, Paris.

Delacroix painted at least three pictures of this subject, taken from *Hamlet*, Act IV, Scene 7. The present version is even more sketchy and typical of Delacroix's later style than the picture in Munich, and it is possible that it was really painted in 1853. Robaut praised the muted colours as a good interpretation of Shakespeare. Some of the studies for this work were done in the grounds of Valmont Abbey, near where Delacroix stayed with relations from time to time, but they are more naturalistic than the finished work.

Plate 36 *The Sultan of Morocco Surrounded by his Court.* 1845. 15 × 13 ½ in. (37.7 × 34 cm.). Musée des Augustins, Toulouse.

According to the note in the catalogue of the 1845 Salon, this picture reproduces exactly the ceremonial Delacroix saw at Meknes when the Sultan received the Comte de Mornay in March, 1832. There are numerous studies, some in pen or water-colour, probably made on the spot, at least one large oil-study and three variants. This might be termed one of Delacroix's Classical works; the Sultan, the only figure on horseback, is endowed with a sculptural solemnity, and the picture is given breadth by the massive walls in the background. It has been suggested that Delacroix was here inspired by one of his own drawings *Duquesclin au château de Pontorson*, and perhaps by an engraving made by Theodore Fielding after Richard Westhall's *Wellington's Entry into Toulouse*. Baudelaire, in his *Salon of 1845*, wrote: 'In spite of the splendour of its hues, this picture is so harmonious that it is grey — as grey as nature, as grey as the atmosphere of summer . . . The composition is excellent; it has an element of the unexpected because it is true and natural.'

Plate 37 *Virgil Presenting Dante to Homer.* 1845-7. Cupola of the Library in the Palais du Luxembourg, Paris.

Villot, in a letter to Alfred Sensier, said that the idea of this subject for the cupola came to Delacroix when he came to tell Villot of his new commission and found him reading Dante. Like Mantegna and Correggio, Delacroix grouped his figures around the base, leaving a central space for clouds and flying figures. In order that they should not give the impression of falling forwards, he worked out their position with a small wooden model. The painter had considerable trouble with this work, partly owing to ill-health. To Planche he said he was painting an Elysium where great poets and sages 'enjoy a happiness which is not merely trivial'. Planche himself, Thoré and Gautier all praised the final work, rightly observing that it was inspired more by the Venetians than by the Florentine or Roman school; others noticed that the painter had managed to compensate for the lack of light given by the architect to the building, and compared the work favourably with Ingres's *Apotheosis of Homer*. In 1868 the canvases which made up the cupola came apart and their repair, undertaken by Delacroix's pupil Andrieu, took fourteen months.

Plate 38 *Othello and Desdemona.* 1847-8. 21 ¾ × 23 ½ in. (50 × 60 cm.). Collection E.V. Thaw, New York.

Delacroix was probably inspired both by Shakespeare's play, which he saw in London in 1825 acted by Kean, and by Rossini's opera, which he saw with Mme de Forget in 1847 itself. The harp on the floor and the lamp held by Othello derive from the opera. A later picture shows Desdemona cursed by her father. There is a drawing for this work and also for another picture showing Desdemona in her room. Although it was shown in the same Salon of 1849 with the second version of the *Women of Algiers*, it still attracted considerable praise and attention for its tragic contrast with the calm languor of the Algerian scene.

Plate 39 *The Triumph of Apollo.* 1850-1. Sketch for the ceiling of the Galerie d'Apollon, Louvre. 51 ½ × 38 ¼ in. (130 × 97 cm.). Musées Royaux des Beaux-Arts de Belgique, Brussels.

Delacroix was here faced with inserting the most important missing part of a scheme conceived by Le Brun. He made innumerable drawings, some impetuous and like Rubens or Tiepolo, and studies, including this, the final one, which shows that he also studied the surrounding ornaments in order to achieve harmony. Delacroix respected Le Brun and realised that his own work would be in a highly important position, open to the most severe criticism. In fact the critics were almost unanimous in praising it. Apollo, of course, was often used in the literature and art of Louis XIV's time as a personification of the monarch and a compliment to him.

Plate 40 *Peace Descends to the Earth bringing Abundance.* 1852. Sketch for ceiling of the Salon de la Paix, Hôtel de Ville, Paris. Diameter 31 in. (78 cm.). Musée Carnavalet, Paris. All the paintings in the Salon de la Paix were destroyed by fire in 1871, but this sketch gives some idea of their composition. Delacroix worked on this ceiling immediately after the Louvre and wrote to George Sand that every morning he would run in excitement to see his work of the previous day. When it was in place on the ceiling, however, he was extremely disappointed and had to repaint it considerably, partly because the room was extremely dark. In this commission Delacroix was assisted by Andrieu.

Plate 41 *Study of Fruit and Flowers.* 1848. 25 ⅞ × 31 ½ in. (65 × 85 cm.). National Gallery, London. Delacroix was a fine painter of flower pieces in the late 40s, when he became more interested in nature. This seems to be an early experiment in the series of still-lifes painted between 1848-50. He was forced to paint in haste and complained in his letters that if he did not his models perished. This study was owned first by Degas and then by Renoir.

Plate 42 *The Sea at Dieppe.* 1852. 14 ¼ × 20 ½ in. (36 × 52 cm.). Ex Collection Beurdeley, Paris. According to the Journal, Delacroix made a sketch from memory on the last day of his visit to Dieppe in September 1852, which seems to correspond with this picture. Towards the end of his life he became very much attracted to such seaside places, which, he wrote, reminded him of Valmont where he had enjoyed good times staying with relations. Although he admitted that without company he would soon be bored and return to Paris, the record of this visit shows that he stayed on the pier for four hours watching the waves break in fury. The careful treatment of light and atmosphere here (though not, of course, the brush-stroke) seems to anticipate the early Impressionism of the next decade.

Plate 43 *Christ on the Sea of Galilee.* c. 1853 19 ¾ × 24 in. (50 × 61 cm.). Dr Fritz Nathan, Zurich. Delacroix had always been interested in the theme of storms and of human beings at the mercy of the elements. In the early 1850s he did at least seven paintings of *Christ on the Sea of Galilee*, some of them showing a rowing boat, some a sailing boat. He was able to combine Baroque and Neo-Classical elements very harmoniously and these pictures were popular with private collectors and dealers. It is sometimes suggested that Delacroix had memories here of Etty's *Storm*, which he had seen on his English visit thirty years before.

Plate 44 *Perseus and Andromeda.* 1853. 17 ⅜ × 13 ½ in. (43.7 × 34.5 cm.). Staatsgalerie, Stuttgart. In Greek mythology Andromeda was the daughter of Cepheus, King of Ethiopia. When her mother boasted that she was more beautiful than the Nereids, Poseidon sent a sea-monster to lay waste the country, but promised deliverance if Andromeda was sacrificed to the monster. She was chained to a rock, but freed by Perseus, who married her. Delacroix may have been inspired by engravings of Titian's *Perseus and Andromeda*, now in the Wallace Collection. The following year Delacroix did a picture on a similar theme, *St. George rescuing* *the Princess*, and he had, of course, already treated the downfall of a monster in the Apollo ceiling. The figure of Perseus whirling down from the sky recurs in the *Heliodorus* of St. Sulpice.

Plate 45 *The Lion Hunt*. 1855. 102 × 141 in. (260 × 359 cm.). Musée des Beaux Arts, Bordeaux.
Delacroix, who had written 'There is in me some black depth which must be appeased', enjoyed depicting the savagery of wild animals, a theme which also combined reminiscences of Rubens and of Morocco. These pictures culminated in this large and whirling *Lion Hunt*, now partially destroyed by fire. A brilliantly-coloured oil study shows the basic rhythm of the picture. Delacroix studied wild animals with careful naturalism in the Jardin des Plantes.

Plate 46 *The Abduction of Rebecca*. 1856-8. 41 ¼ × 32 in. (105 × 81.5 cm.). Musée du Louvre, Paris.
This was probably begun at Champrosay in the spring of 1856. The theme is taken from Walter Scott's *Ivanhoe*, and shows Rebecca carried from Front-de-Boeuf's castle by the Templar, Bois-Guilbert. There is another version, painted in 1846, and also pictures of the wounded Ivanhoe and Rebecca, where she is reporting on the state of the battle from the castle. This picture was shown at the Salon of 1859, and provoked harsh criticisms as had his previous picture of Rebecca, for being unfinished.

Plate 47 *Ovid Among the Scythians*. 1859. 34 ½ × 51 ¼ in. (88 × 136 cm.). National Gallery, London.
Augustus banished Ovid from Italy in 8 A.D. This work is characteristic of Delacroix's late pastoral pictures, which are somewhat loosely constructed, with landscapes almost as prominent as the figures. It also treats one of his favourite themes, genius ill-treated by the powerful. The subject was first used for one of the pendentives in the Library of the Palais-Bourbon, and there is also an oil sketch for this picture and a smaller version with variations painted in 1862. Lee Johnson shows that some of the figures go back to 1821.

Plate 48 *Horses Emerging from the Sea*. 1860. 20 × 24 in. (50 × 61 cm.). Phillips Collection, Washington.
This picture, commissioned by the dealer Estienne, was probably begun in 1858, and in some ways is a souvenir of his visit to Africa thirty years before, since it shows a Moroccan rider and town on the far shore — although Delacroix originally wrote of it as 'a view of Dieppe'. The rhythm of the horses' necks and the rider is masterly. After the painter's death in 1873, it was engraved by Languillermie for a sale.

Plate 49 *Jacob Wrestling with the Angel* (detail). 1856-61. Oil and wax on plaster. 281 × 191 in. (714 × 488 cm.). Church of Saint-Sulpice, Paris.
This work, which symbolises and crowns Delacroix's struggles as an artist, suffered many setbacks, originally from a mistake which led Delacroix to suppose that he was painting in a baptismal chapel, and later from the painter's many attacks of illness. At one time he commuted between his country home at Champrosay and the chapel every day, but at the end of 1857 he moved to the Place Furstenberg in order to be nearer his work. In this year Delacroix wrote in his Journal: 'I like churches, I like being alone in them and sitting down quietly and having a good long meditation.' The *Jacob* and the other picture *Heliodorus expelled from the Temple* were painted directly on to the walls with a mixture of wax and oil paints. The four pendentives are decorated by grisaille angels. Delacroix did not altogether exclude grey and earth colours from these decorations, but he generally used them behind the principal figures as a foil for the bright colours. The composition and mood of this work owed much to Titian's *Death of St. Peter Martyr* for Santi Giovanni e Paolo.

1

2

3

4

5

6

8

9

12

13

14

15

16

19

20

24

25

26

27

28

32

34

35

40

41

43

47

48

49